MASTERCHEF
1993

MASTER
1993
CHEF

MASTERCHEF 1993

FOREWORD BY LOYD GROSSMAN

GENERAL EDITOR: JANET ILLSLEY

VERMILLION
LONDON

First published 1993

13 5 7 9 10 8 6 4 2

First published in the United Kingdom in 1993 by
Vermilion
Random House, 20 Vauxhall Bridge Road, London SW1V 2SA

Random House Australia (Pty) Limited
20 Alfred Street, Milsons Point, Sydney,
New South Wales 2061, Australia

Random House New Zealand Limited
18 Poland Road, Glenfield
Auckland 10, New Zealand

Random House South Africa (Pty) Limited
PO Box 337, Bergvlei, South Africa

Random House UK Limited Reg. No. 954009

A CIP catalogue record for this book is available
from the British Library

MasterChef 1993
A Union Pictures production for BBC North
Series devised by Franc Roddam
Executive Producer: Bradley Adams
Producer and Director: Richard Bryan
Production Manager: Fiona Reid
Production Co-ordinator: Melanie Jappy

General Editor: Janet Illsley
Design: Clive Dorman

ISBN: 0 09 177765 8

Typeset by Clive Dorman & Co.
Printed and bound in Great Britain by Butler & Tanner Ltd,
Frome and London, using environmentally friendly inks.

CONTENTS

FOREWORD

I "modestly" feel that MasterChef is the best and most entertaining programme about food that's ever been broadcast in Britain, but I also have a hunch that in the future it will be prized as a social document and a witness to the years when Great Britain fell in love with food. The MasterChef saga began when Franc Roddam who created the show was living in Los Angeles and getting rather fed up with listening to clichéd diatribes about how frightful British food was. MasterChef was devised to dazzle the doomsayers with the excellence of British cooking. Thankfully it did and for the last four years the judges and I have been consistently thrilled with, and gratified by, not only the cooking on offer but also by the inventiveness, the skill and the downright joy of all our contestants.

Anyone who's followed the programme will have noted that we cast a broad net when it comes to seeking out contestants. Of course, at the end of our regional cook-offs, it is the best cooks and only the best cooks who are asked to go forward to the televised competition. But gratifyingly the best cooks have come in all ages, shapes and sizes, and from all walks of life. Almost needless to say they have come in both sexes as well. When the competition began we were surprised at how many men rushed to fill in their application forms. By this year roughly equal numbers of men and women were entering and, in a vivid contrast to 1992's all women final, this year our three finalists were men. What that means to me and perhaps to future social historians is that in 1993 we might have witnessed a public realisation that good food is for everyone. I've always liked to think that MasterChef has tried to break down some of the misconceptions about food that exist in Britain, including ideas that good food has anything to do with class, money, pretention or indeed gender. I warmly welcome Derek Johns into the MasterChefs' circle. He is a brilliant cook and a great winner. Will he be the first of many male MasterChefs?

As always, the cooking of all our contestants continues to enthral. This year forceful, earthy, "real" flavours have again dominated the competition. In the past we've mentioned that you have to be a good eater first in order to be a good cook. I feel I ought to add that you have to be a good shopper too, and our contestants were brilliant shoppers. They bought their raw materials with real love and devotion, and sometimes with a scholarly touch as well. All the judges and I were excited to see so many great local products being used so well. We were also all surprised by rabbit's new-found popularity. And whenever I thought that no pudding would ever taste as good as the one I'd just sampled ... along came another wonder! There are some desiderata though. I would still like to see more vegetarian cooks staking their claims to MasterChef status and I would welcome more cooks from all the culinarily exciting ethnic communities in Britain. And please can we have some more traditional British regional dishes too...

I owe my greatest debt to all our contestants who make MasterChef so exciting and compelling for me, and I hope for you. Once again I am more than grateful to Franc Roddam, to Brad Adams our executive producer, to Richard Bryan our producer director, to our beloved floor manager "Fizz" Waters and to the rest of the MasterChef team for helping to make such a great, uplifting programme.

Loyd Grossman

NOTES FOR RECIPE USERS

Quantities are given in metric and imperial measures.
Follow one set of measurements only, not a combination,
because they are not interchangeable.

All spoon measures are level.

Fresh herbs are used unless otherwise stated.

Ovens must be preheated to the temperature
specified in the recipe.

All recipes serve 4.

INTRODUCTION

This is the fourth book of recipes from the MasterChef competition and, as always, it is full of exciting and incredibly creative dishes. It has been a stimulating and hard-fought contest. Vanessa Binns, our 1992 winner, has handed over her trophy to Derek Johns, the first ever male MasterChef, and once more our crew have packed away their forks, always kept at the ready, for another year.

Our 1993 guest judges, who have shared with Loyd Grossman the almost impossible task of choosing between the offerings of the red, yellow and blue kitchens, have been a blend of old friends and exciting new faces. The final has by coincidence – or has it become a tradition – always been judged by a gastronomic knight: Sir Roy Strong, Sir Clement Freud, Sir Terence Conran and this year someone who clearly delights in his food, Sir John Harvey-Jones; he was joined by another old friend, Michel Roux.

We were thrilled to lure from his home in New York, Robert Carrier, who with Jane Grigson and Elizabeth David, first interested this nation of meat-and-two-veg eaters in the possibility of bringing the tastes of Europe into its kitchen. In contrast we were delighted to welcome some of Britain's most exciting young chefs to judge for us: Gary Rhodes, David Burke and Anthony Worrall-Thompson; as well as food writers Josceline Dimbleby, Leslie Forbes and Valentina Harris.

"Oh I am glad I came!" exclaimed Michael Elphick as he tucked in to his third dinner of the evening. I think this sentiment would be true of all our judges who can clearly be seen to be enjoying the wonderfully imaginative dishes which our contestants have presented. And now it is your turn. We all hope that both the MasterChef programme and this collection of the recipes contribute to making your time in the kitchen, and at the table, even more enjoyable.

RICHARD BRYAN
Producer and Director
MasterChef

REGIONAL HEATS
THE MIDLANDS
BRIAN TOMPKINS • ANGELA GEARY • ALASTAIR HENDY

WINNER

BRIAN TOMPKINS' MENU

STARTER
*Light Clear Fish Broth, enriched with White Wine
and Peppercorns*

"THIS LIGHT CLEAR FISH BROTH WAS PERFECTION. DEFINITELY TEN
OUT OF TEN" ROBERT CARRIER

MAIN COURSE
*Walnut-coated Best End of Manx Lochtan Lamb, served
with a Stock Ale Sauce and Pickled Walnuts
Garlic Potato Streamers
Glazed Radishes
Polish-style Curly Kale*

"THE DISPLAY WAS WONDERFUL TO LOOK AT. THE WHOLE THING HAD A
TREMENDOUS APPEARANCE TO IT" MICHAEL ELPHICK

DESSERT
*Sweet Pieroszki, filled with Ricotta Cheese and Candied Citrus
Zests, served on a Citrus Caramel*

Brian Tompkins lives in Great Brington in Northamptonshire
with his wife Nicky, and sons Ben and Danny. Brian is
an optometrist with a thriving practice in Northampton.
Essentially a family man, Brian enjoys spending time with
his children. Both Brian and Nicky are involved in village life –
they both took part in the village pantomime last year.

LIGHT CLEAR FISH BROTH, ENRICHED WITH WHITE WINE AND PEPPERCORNS

If gurnard is not available, you can use any flavoursome fish for this light broth, such as salmon trout.

2 leeks
2 celery sticks
½ large sweet onion
175 ml (6 fl oz) dry white wine
2 gurnard, each about 625 g (1¼ lb), filleted
   (bones, heads and trimmings reserved for
   stock)
2 egg whites
5 green peppercorns
1-2 dill sprigs

To Serve:
20 ml (4 tsp) pink peppercorns
salt
15-30 ml (1-2 tbsp) grated cucumber

Either cut the vegetables into julienne strips or roughly chop them in a food processor. Pour the wine into a pan and boil steadily to reduce by half. Add the prepared vegetables, cover and cook gently until softened.

Trim the fish fillets and cut neat diamond shapes for the garnish; set aside. Reserve all the trimmings.

Put about 1.5 litres (2½ pints) water in a large pan and add all the fish bones and trimmings, including the heads. Heat gently until almost boiling. Add the vegetables and wine, and simmer very gently for no more than 20 minutes, skimming as necessary.

Strain the liquid through a fine sieve lined with muslin into a bowl and allow to settle. Ladle out the clear broth, leaving any residue in the bottom of the bowl. (Keep the fish and vegetable mixture for clarifying the stock.)

Transfer 300 ml (½ pint) of this stock to a clean pan and heat to a simmer.

Add the diamonds of fish and poach gently for 3 minutes; remove and reserve. Skim the poaching liquid and add to the strained stock.

To clarify the stock, finely chop about 15 ml (1 tbsp) of the reserved fish and vegetable mixture and mix with the egg whites. Slowly bring the stock to the boil in a large pan, whisking in the egg white mixture. Lower the heat and simmer for about 30 minutes. As the egg whites cook, they rise to the top of the pan drawing up any impurities to form a froth on the surface, and leaving the stock beneath clear and sparkling. Carefully remove the frothy layer, then ladle the soup through a muslin-lined sieve into a clean pan.

Reduce the stock by boiling to about 600 ml (1 pint). Add the green peppercorns and dill sprigs and simmer gently for 10 minutes, then strain.

To serve, add the pink peppercorns to the soup and season with salt to taste. Reheat gently, then pour into warmed soup bowls and float a diamond of fish fillet in the centre of each portion. Scatter the grated cucumber around the fish. Serve hot or chilled.

WALNUT-COATED BEST END OF MANX LOCHTAN LAMB

Lochtan lamb is a wonderful 'gamey' lean meat from a four-horned breed reared on an organic farm on the Isle of Man. You could however use traditional English or Welsh Lamb. Ask your butcher for some extra lamb bones if possible to use as a trivet for roasting the lamb. Get your butcher to 'French trim' the lamb, removing all bones except the 'fingers' of the rib bones for decoration.

2 best ends of lamb
a little extra virgin olive oil
beaten egg yolk, for brushing

Coating:
100-175 g (4-6 oz) walnut halves
50 g (2 oz) brown sugar
15 ml (1 tbsp) chopped parsley

Sauce:
600 ml (1 pint) gamey lamb stock (see right)
15 ml (1 tbsp) good malty real ale
salt and freshly ground black pepper
knob of butter, to thicken

To Garnish:
3-4 firm pickled walnuts
flat-leaved parsley

To prepare the lamb, scrape the ribs until they are completely clean to avoid any scraps of tissue burning.

Put all the ingredients for the coating in a food processor and process until the mixture resembles fine crumbs, then spread out on a large plate.

Heat a little olive oil in a frying pan and sear the lamb joints on all sides, then place on the trivet of extra bones (or on a metal trivet) in a roasting tin. Roast in a preheated oven at 220°C (425°F) mark 7 for 8-10 minutes, then remove and brush the meat (not the rib bones) with egg yolk. Holding the rib bones, dip the meat in the walnut mixture to coat evenly. Put back on the trivet and roast for a further 8-10 minutes (depending on the size of the joint and how pink you like your lamb).

While the lamb is cooking, reduce the lamb stock by boiling until it is thick enough to coat the back of a spoon. Just before serving, add the ale and season well with salt and pepper. Remove from the heat and whisk in the butter. Keep warm.

Cover the lamb with foil and leave to rest for 5 minutes, then carve into cutlets. Arrange these on hot serving plates, spoon the sauce over the meat and garnish with sliced pickled walnuts and flat-leaved parsley.

Gamey Lamb Stock: Prepare this in advance. You will need 1 kg (2 lb) 'gamey' lamb bones, or include a pheasant carcass if using a domestic breed of lamb. Place in a roasting tin with 1 onion, quartered; 1 carrot, quartered lengthways; 1 leek, roughly chopped; and 2 tomatoes, halved. Roast at 200°C (400°F) mark 6 for about 15 minutes until well browned.

Transfer the bones and vegetables to a large saucepan and add 5 pints (3 litres) water, salt and a bouquet garni. Bring to the boil and simmer gently for 3-4 hours, skimming from time to time. Strain through a fine sieve and allow to cool. Chill, then remove any fat from the surface. Return to a clean pan and reduce to about 600 ml (1 pint) by boiling to concentrate the flavour.

GARLIC POTATO STREAMERS

4 large Desirée potatoes, peeled
125 g (4 oz) unsalted butter
4 cloves garlic, crushed
salt and freshly ground black pepper
freshly grated Parmesan cheese, for
  sprinkling

Cut the potatoes crosswise into 2.5 cm (1 inch) thick slices. Using a potato peeler, carefully peel around the potato slices to form long ribbons or 'streamers'. Immerse in a bowl of iced water and leave to soak for 1 hour.

Meanwhile melt the butter in a pan, add the garlic and soften gently to flavour the butter. Remove the potato streamers from the water and pat dry on kitchen paper.

Dip the potato streamers in the garlic butter and place on a baking sheet. Season with salt and pepper and sprinkle with a little Parmesan. Roast in a preheated oven at 200°C (400°F) mark 6, for about 12-15 minutes until golden. Serve immediately.

GLAZED RADISHES

36 small radishes
50 g (2 oz) butter
salt and freshly ground black pepper
5 ml (1 tsp) sugar

Trim the radishes, leaving the root points and a short stalk on each one. Place in a small pan with the butter, salt and pepper, and the sugar. Add enough water to half-cover the radishes and bring to the boil. Lower the heat and simmer for about 10 minutes until the water is reduced and the butter coats the radishes in a shiny glaze. Serve at once.

POLISH-STYLE CURLY KALE

25 g (1 oz) butter
5 ml (1 tsp) caraway seeds
1 egg
350 g (12 oz) curly kale
salt and freshly ground black pepper
15 ml (1 tbsp) chopped parsley

Melt the butter in a pan, remove from the heat, add the caraway seeds and set aside to allow the flavours to mingle. Hard-boil the egg; drain and cool under cold running water. Bring 1.2 litres (2 pints) water to the boil in a saucepan, add the curly kale and cook for 3-4 minutes. Drain and immediately refresh with cold water. Drain thoroughly and set aside.

To reheat, place the kale in an oven-proof bowl, add the caraway butter and turn the kale to coat with the butter. Season with salt and pepper. Place in a preheated oven at 200°C (400°F) mark 6 for 3-4 minutes.

Meanwhile, shell the egg. Finely chop or grate the egg white and mix with the chopped parsley. Press the egg yolk through a fine sieve.

Serve the kale sprinkled with the egg white and, finally, the sieved egg yolk.

SWEET PIEROSZKI FILLED WITH RICOTTA CHEESE AND CANDIED CITRUS ZESTS ON A CITRUS CARAMEL

Pieroszki:
225 g (8 oz) plain flour
pinch of salt
150 g (5 oz) unsalted butter, cubed
1 egg, size 2
15 ml (1 tbsp) soured cream
a little lime juice, for brushing
125 g (4 oz) ricotta cheese
15 ml (1 tbsp) caster sugar
15 ml (1 tbsp) sultanas soaked in 10 ml
   (2 tsp) Grand Marnier
5 ml (1 tsp) lime juice
300 ml (½ pint) sunflower oil, for frying

Candied Citrus Zests:
2 limes
1 large orange
125 g (4 oz) caster sugar

Citrus Caramel:
125 g (4 oz) caster sugar
juice of ½ lime
15 ml (1 tbsp) orange juice
7.5 ml (1½ tsp) Grand Marnier
30 ml (2 tbsp) double cream
50 g (2 oz) clarified butter

To Serve:
icing sugar, for dusting
orange and lime segments

To make the pieroszki dough, put the flour and salt in a food processor with the butter and process until the mixture resembles fine crumbs. Add the egg and soured cream and process briefly until the dough holds together. Turn onto a lightly floured surface and knead gently for 5 minutes. Wrap and leave to rest in the refrigerator for 30 minutes.

To prepare the candied citrus zests, finely pare the rind of the limes and orange using a zester, then blanch in boiling water for 8 minutes; drain. Put the sugar and 100 ml (3½ fl oz) water in a pan and heat gently until dissolved. Add the citrus zests and boil steadily for 3 minutes. Leave to cool in the syrup, then remove with a slotted spoon. Chop 15 ml (1 tbsp) for the filling; set aside the rest for decoration.

To prepare the filling, in a bowl mix the ricotta cheese with the sugar, 15 ml (1 tbsp) candied citrus zest, sultanas in Grand Marnier and lime juice; set aside.

To shape the pieroszki, roll out the dough on a floured surface to a 5 mm (¼ inch) thickness. Using a 7.5 cm (3 inch) cutter, cut out about 18 circles of dough and moisten the edges with a little lime juice. Place about 5 ml (1 tsp) of filling on one half of each dough circle, fold over the other half to enclose the filling and crimp the edges with a fork to seal.

Cook the pieroszki in batches. Drop a few into a pan of boiling water, stir gently to prevent sticking, and simmer gently for 3-4 minutes or until they float to the surface. Remove with a slotted spoon and cool on an oiled plate.

Meanwhile make the citrus caramel. Put the sugar and 60 ml (2 fl oz) water in a heavy-based pan and heat gently until dissolved, then increase the heat and cook until the syrup is golden. Remove from the heat and carefully add the lime and orange juices and Grand Marnier. Stir until smooth, then stir in the cream. Finally, stir in the butter to glaze; keep warm.

Heat the sunflower oil in a deep frying pan and fry the pieroszki for a few minutes on each side until crisp and golden. Drain on kitchen paper, then dust liberally with icing sugar.

To serve, cover each plate with citrus caramel. Arrange 3 or 4 of the best pieroszki on each plate. Place orange and lime segments between them and top with candied citrus zests.

REGIONAL HEATS
THE MIDLANDS
BRIAN TOMPKINS • ANGELA GEARY • ALASTAIR HENDY

ANGELA GEARY'S MENU

STARTER
Tabbouleh with Spicy Prawns

MAIN COURSE
Tuna with Peppercorns in a Port Wine Sauce
Tomato and Basil Salad
New Potatoes

"THE TUNA WAS A REAL SUCCESS, REALLY UNUSUAL AND MARVELLOUSLY GAMEY. LOVELY SAUCE AS WELL" ROBERT CARRIER

DESSERT
Honey and Apple Charlottes, served with Cider and Apple Brandy Cream

"THIS MENU IS SIMPLE, FRESH, RICH AND SEXY, WITH GREAT COLOURS AND A HOMEMADE LOOK WITH A TOUCH OF NOUVELLE CUISINE" ROBERT CARRIER

Angela Geary comes from Nottingham. Angela is an active member of the local Women's Institute and regularly helps at their Friday market in the town's YMCA. Her other hobbies include knitting and gardening. Angela also enjoys spending time with her godson, Alexander.

TABBOULEH WITH SPICY PRAWNS

125 g (4 oz) fine couscous
juice of 3 limes
½ small green pepper
1 tomato
1 shallot, or ½ small onion
30-45 ml (2-3 tbsp) chopped parsley
30-45 ml (2-3 tbsp) chopped mint
salt and freshly ground black pepper
30 ml (2 tbsp) olive oil

Prawns:

225 g (8 oz) large raw prawns, in their
   shells
25 g (1 oz) butter
1.25 ml (¼ tsp) harissa sauce, or cayenne
   pepper

To Garnish:

flat-leaved parsley sprigs

Put the couscous into a large bowl (which allows plenty of room for the grains to swell). Stir in the lime juice and leave for 1 hour for the grains to absorb the lime juice, soften and swell. Stir well with a fork to break up any lumps. If the mixture is too dry, add a little water.

Finely dice the green pepper; seed and dice the tomato; chop the onion very finely. Add the pepper, tomato and shallot to the couscous. Stir in the chopped parsley and mint. Season with salt and pepper to taste and stir in the olive oil. Cover and chill before serving.

Shell the prawns, leaving the tails on if preferred. Heat the butter in a frying pan and when sizzling, add the prawns. Lower the heat and stir the prawns until they turn pink and opaque.

Stir in the harissa a little at a time, tasting as you go – take care, it is very hot! Transfer the mixture to a bowl and leave until cold.

To serve, place a portion of the tabbouleh on one side of a small serving plate and arrange the prawn mixture on the other side. Garnish with flat-leaved parsley.

Note: If raw prawns are not available, use ready-cooked prawns but heat them through only briefly or they will become rubbery and unpleasant to eat.

TUNA WITH PEPPERCORNS IN A PORT WINE SAUCE

I prefer to use a tuna steak, cut from a large fish. If unavailable, you can use two smaller steaks, each about 350 g (12 oz) in weight.

*1 fresh tuna steak, about 700 g (1½ lb) and
    3 cm (1¼ inch) thick
15 ml (1 tbsp) black peppercorns
15 ml (1 tbsp) plain flour
salt
15 ml (1 tbsp) oil
50 g (2 oz) butter
30 ml (2 tbsp) brandy*

Sauce:
*150 ml (¼ pint) ruby port
475 ml (16 fl oz) good chicken stock
150 ml (¼ pint) double cream*

First prepare the tuna. Using a sharp knife, remove the tough outer skin and the large central bone from the steak. Discard any long bones around the stomach cavity of the fish steak too. The steak will separate neatly into 4 quarters, each providing a portion.

Coarsely crush the peppercorns using a pestle and mortar. Mix with the flour and a little salt. Use to coat the tuna pieces thoroughly.

Heat the oil and butter in a heavy-based pan, which is large enough to hold the pieces of fish in a single layer. When sizzling, add the tuna and cook over a brisk heat, turning to brown both sides. Heat the brandy in a small pan until the vapour rises, then set alight and pour it, flaming, over the tuna. Shake the pan and tilt it to ensure the flames reach all parts of the pan.

When the flames die down deglaze the pan with the port, stirring well to scrape up the sediment. Simmer over a low heat for 10-15 minutes until the fish is cooked through and flakes easily. Lift the tuna portions from the pan with a fish slice and transfer to a hot plate; keep warm.

Place the frying pan over a high heat, add the stock and boil vigorously to reduce the liquid to a thick, syrupy consistency. Stir in the cream and simmer for a few minutes to reduce; the sauce should be fairly thick but still pourable.

Place the tuna steaks on hot serving plates and pour around a little of the sauce. Serve immediately, with new potatoes and the tomato and basil salad.

TOMATO AND BASIL SALAD

This salad should be left at room temperature – not in the refrigerator for at least 1 hour before serving to allow the flavours to develop.

*4 tomatoes
salt and freshly ground black pepper
30-45 ml (2-3 tbsp) finely shredded basil
30 ml (2 tbsp) red wine vinegar
60 ml (4 tbsp) olive oil
basil sprigs, to garnish*

Slice the tomatoes, season with salt and pepper to taste and layer in a bowl with the shredded basil.

In a small bowl, whisk together the vinegar and oil, season and pour over the tomatoes, turning them carefully once or twice to ensure they are well coated with dressing.

Cover and set aside for at least 1 hour before serving.

HONEY APPLE CHARLOTTES, WITH CIDER AND APPLE BRANDY CREAM

For these charlottes you will need 4 individual straight-sided moulds, about 200 ml (7 fl oz) capacity. I use small cleaned baked bean tins!

Charlottes:
900 g (2 lb) dessert apples (Cox's or Royal Gala)
30 ml (2 tbsp) clear honey
175 g (6 oz) butter
a little ground cinnamon, to taste
1 small white loaf (preferably 2-3 days old)

Cider and Apple Brandy Cream:
300 ml (½ pint) dry cider
150 ml (¼ pint) double cream
20 ml (4 tsp) Somerset apple brandy, or Calvados
10 ml (2 tsp) clear honey

To Decorate:
1 red-skinned dessert apple
50 g (2 oz) granulated sugar
4 mint sprigs

Peel, core and thickly slice the apples. Put the apple slices in a pan with the honey and 25 g (1 oz) of the butter and bring to a simmer, stirring occasionally. Cook gently for about 15 minutes until the apples are soft and all the liquid in the pan has evaporated; check carefully at this stage to make sure the apples do not catch and burn. Turn the cooked apples into a bowl, stir in the cinnamon to taste, and set aside.

Slice the bread fairly thinly and remove the crusts. Cut out 8 circles to fit the base of the moulds, then cut 2.5 cm (1 inch) strips to line the sides.

Melt the remaining 150 g (5 oz) butter, then dip the bread into the butter to coat. Use four of the circles to line the base of the moulds and use the strips to line the sides, trimming them so they fit snugly with no gaps or overlaps.

Spoon the apple mixture into the lined moulds – be generous! Cover with the remaining 4 circles of bread. Place on a baking sheet and bake in a preheated oven at 200°C (400°F) mark 6 for 30 minutes until golden and crisp.

Meanwhile, prepare the cider and apple brandy cream. Put the cider in a pan, bring to the boil and boil vigorously to reduce until only 30 ml (2 tbsp) remains; it will be thick and syrupy at this stage. Allow to cool, then add to the double cream, mixing well; this thickens the cream so that it is firm enough to pipe without whipping. Stir in the apple brandy and honey and chill until required.

To prepare the decoration, quarter and core the unpeeled red apple, then cut into thin slices. Dissolve the sugar in 125 ml (4 fl oz) water in a pan over a low heat, then boil steadily for 3 minutes to make a sugar syrup. Add the apple slices and poach gently for about 5 minutes until barely tender. Remove with a slotted spoon and drain.

To serve, spoon or pipe a generous swirl of cider cream on one side of each serving plate. Turn out a hot apple charlotte and arrange alongside but not touching the cream. Decorate with a fan of poached apple spices and a mint sprig. Serve immediately.

REGIONAL HEATS
THE MIDLANDS

BRIAN TOMPKINS • ANGELA GEARY • ALASTAIR HENDY

ALASTAIR HENDY'S MENU

STARTER

*Warm Salad of Wild Mushrooms with Deep-fried Polenta
and Balsamic Dressing*

MAIN COURSE

*Red Mullet and Grilled Vegetables, with a Peppered
Fish Sauce and Rouille*

*"THIS DISH IS A TRIUMPH. IT LOOKS SO COLOURFUL... IT LOOKS ALMOST
LIKE AN ACTION PAINTING" LOYD*

DESSERT

*Caramelised Rice Pudding and Pears, with a
Gingered Caramel Sauce*

Alastair Hendy from Eydon in Northamptonshire works as a photographic stylist, specialising in exotic and elaborate flower displays. A former antiques dealer, he has an impressive collection of Poole pottery from the twenties and thirties. His latest leisure pursuit is scuba diving.

WARM SALAD OF WILD MUSHROOMS WITH DEEP-FRIED POLENTA AND BALSAMIC DRESSING

Use whichever wild mushrooms are in season for this salad, such as chanterelles, hedgehog mushrooms, horn of plenty, and oyster mushrooms.

Polenta:

900 ml (1½ pints) salted water
150 g (5 oz) polenta
25 g (1 oz) butter
25 g (1 oz) freshly grated Parmesan cheese
oil for deep-frying

Salad:

175 g (6 oz) young spinach leaves
1 bunch rocket leaves
22 ml (1½ tbsp) olive oil
25 g (1 oz) butter
275 g (10 oz) wild mushrooms, cleaned
1 large clove garlic, chopped
15 ml (1 tbsp) chopped flat-leaved parsley
salt and freshly ground black pepper

To Serve:

12 ml (½ tbsp) balsamic vinegar
30 ml (2 tbsp) extra-virgin olive oil
freshly shredded Parmesan cheese

First make the polenta. Bring the salted water to the boil in a pan and slowly trickle in the polenta, whisking continuously until evenly combined and smooth. Lower the heat and cook, stirring continuously with a wooden spoon, for 30-40 minutes, making sure the polenta does not stick to the base of the pan. The polenta is cooked when it leaves the sides of the pan clean.

Stir in the butter and grated Parmesan and pour into a shallow square dish. Allow to cool for about 30 minutes until set, then cut into 1 cm (½ inch) cubes.

Heat the oil in a deep-fat fryer. When it is hot, deep-fry the polenta cubes in batches until crisp and golden. Drain on kitchen paper. Combine the spinach and rocket in a large salad bowl.

Heat the olive oil and butter in a frying pan and sauté the mushrooms and garlic over a moderate to high heat for 2-3 minutes. Remove from the heat, stir in the parsley and seasoning to taste, then spoon over the salad in the bowl.

Add the balsamic vinegar to the pan and heat, stirring to scrape up the sediment, then pour over the salad. Add the polenta cubes, drizzle with the olive oil and adjust the seasoning. Toss the salad gently and serve immediately, topped with slivers of Parmesan cheese.

Red Mullet and Grilled Vegetables, with a Peppered Fish Sauce and Rouille

During the summer when samphire is in season, use it in preference to spinach, making sure it is thoroughly cleaned.

3-4 red mullet, each about 225 g (8 oz), filleted (bones and trimmings reserved for the stock)
salt and freshly ground black pepper
22 ml (1½ tbsp) olive oil

Stock:
fish bones and trimmings from the red mullet
1 onion, quartered
few parsley and thyme sprigs
300 ml (½ pint) dry white wine

Sauce:
30 ml (2 tbsp) olive oil
1 shallot, or ½ small onion, chopped
1 carrot, diced
2 cloves garlic, peeled
30 ml (2 tbsp) chopped flat-leaved parsley
1 bay leaf
30 ml (2 tbsp) tomato purée
large pinch of cayenne pepper, or to taste
600 ml (1 pint) dry white wine

Rouille:
1 red pepper
2 cloves garlic, blanched
5 ml (1 tsp) tomato purée
15 ml (1 tbsp) olive oil
15 ml (1 tbsp) fresh white breadcrumbs
15 ml (1 tbsp) crème fraîche
large pinch of cayenne pepper, or to taste

Vegetables:
2 red peppers
1 aubergine
salt
2 red onions
1 fennel bulb
2 large courgettes
60 ml (4 tbsp) olive oil, flavoured with garlic and herbs to taste

To Serve:
225 g (8 oz) spinach or samphire
black olives, to garnish

Put all the ingredients for the stock in a large pan, bring to the boil, lower the heat and simmer for 15 minutes, skimming frequently. Strain through a fine sieve, then return the stock to the pan and boil to reduce to 150 ml (¼ pint).

To make the sauce, heat the oil in a pan, add the shallot, carrot and garlic cloves and sauté for 2 minutes. Add all the remaining sauce ingredients. Bring to the boil, lower the heat and simmer for 15 minutes, then increase the heat and boil to reduce to 150 ml (¼ pint). Strain through a fine sieve and add the fish stock; set aside.

Season the red mullet fillets with salt and pepper and rub with a little olive oil. If they are large, cut the fillets in half.

Place all 3 red peppers, including the one for the rouille, on a baking sheet, drizzle with a little oil and bake in a preheated oven at 200°C (400°F) mark 6 for 25 minutes. Remove from the oven, place in a dish, cover and leave until cool enough to handle, then peel off the skins. Halve the peppers and discard the cores and seeds.

To make the rouille, put 1 red pepper in a food processor or blender with the blanched garlic and tomato purée and work to a purée. With the motor running, add the oil in a thin steady stream through the feeder tube to form a thick, glossy mixture. Turn into a bowl and fold in the breadcrumbs to thicken the rouille. Add the crème fraîche and season with cayenne pepper and salt to taste.

To prepare the vegetables, slice the aubergine into thick rounds, sprinkle liberally with salt and leave to degorge for at least 20 minutes. Thickly slice the red onions, to give 4 solid rounds from each one. Trim the fennel and cut lengthways into 8 slices. Cut the courgettes into thick slices on the diagonal. Slice the 2 red peppers into strips.

To cook the vegetables, place the onion and fennel slices on a baking sheet, drizzle with 30 ml (2 tbsp) of the flavoured oil and roast in the oven at 180°C (350°F) mark 4 for 20 minutes, turning once. Add the pepper strips for the last 5 minutes.

Rinse the aubergine slices thoroughly in cold water to remove the salt and bitter juices and pat dry with kitchen paper.

Heat a ribbed chargrill pan until smoking hot. Brush the courgette and aubergine slices with a little of the flavoured oil and chargrill in batches until just cooked; keep warm while cooking the remainder. (Alternatively, these can be roasted in the oven with the onions and fennel).

Blanch the spinach in boiling water until just wilted and drain thoroughly, pressing the spinach to squeeze out excess moisture; keep warm. Reheat the fish sauce and keep warm.

To cook the fish, heat 15 ml (1 tbsp) olive oil in a large non-stick frying pan and gently fry the fish fillets, flesh-side down, for 5 minutes, then turn and fry the skin side for 2 minutes.

To serve, place a small mound of spinach in the centre of each warmed serving plate. Arrange a selection of vegetables with the red mullet in a circle on top. Pour the sauce around the fish and vegetables. Add a spoonful of rouille to each portion and garnish with black olives.

CARAMELISED RICE PUDDING AND PEARS, WITH A GINGERED CARAMEL SAUCE

Rice Pudding:
115 g (4½ oz) pudding rice
600 ml (1 pint) milk
½ vanilla pod, split
115 g (4½ oz) caster sugar

Poached Pears:
4 William pears
1 vanilla pod, split
125 g (4 oz) caster sugar
15 ml (1 tbsp) lemon juice
caster sugar, for sprinkling

Custard:
4 egg yolks
15 g (½ oz) caster sugar
175 ml (6 fl oz) milk
½ vanilla pod, split

Caramel:
50 g (2 oz) caster sugar

Ginger Sauce:
2.5 cm (1 inch) piece fresh root ginger,
  peeled and chopped
150 g (5 oz) caster sugar
40 g (1½ oz) unsalted butter

To make the rice pudding, blanch the rice in boiling water for 2 minutes, then drain. Put the milk and vanilla pod in a heavy-based pan and bring to the boil. Add the rice and sugar, stir well and simmer for 30 minutes. Strain through a sieve.

Peel and core the pears. Put them in a pan, add water to cover, then add the vanilla pod, caster sugar and lemon juice. Bring to the boil, lower the heat and gently poach the pears for 20 minutes or until tender. Leave the pears to cool in the syrup.

Meanwhile make the custard, whisk the egg yolks with the sugar in a bowl until pale and creamy. Put the milk and vanilla pod in a saucepan and bring to the boil. Remove from the heat and allow to cool, then whisk into the egg mixture. Strain through a sieve into a bowl and stir in the rice.

To prepare the caramel, put the sugar in a small pan with 30 (2 tbsp) water over a low heat until dissolved, then boil steadily until the syrup turns golden brown. Immediately pour the caramel into the base of the pudding moulds.

Divide the rice and custard mixture between the moulds, place in a roasting tin containing enough water to come halfway up the sides of the moulds. Bake in a preheated oven at 180°C (350°F) mark 4 for 25 minutes or until set.

Meanwhile to make the ginger sauce, put the ginger and sugar in a small pan with 30 ml (2 tbsp) water. Place over a low heat until the sugar is dissolved, then cook until the syrup caramelises. Carefully add the butter and a further 75-90 ml (5-6 tbsp) water a little at a time. Heat gently, stirring, then strain.

Cut the pears into thin slices and place on a baking sheet. Sprinkle liberally with caster sugar. Put under a very hot grill to caramelise the sugar. (Alternatively you can use a blow torch.)

To serve, unmould a rice pudding on to the centre of each serving plate. Surround with the pear slices and gingered caramel sauce.

REGIONAL HEATS

LONDON

ROSS BURDEN • MARWAN BADRAN • AMANDA DAWSON

WINNER

ROSS BURDEN'S MENU

STARTER

Mussels with Saffron in a Light Broth

"THE LOOK OF THE BROTH WAS JUST MARVELLOUS. IT LOOKED
SO HARMONIOUS ... AND I LOVED THE SAFFRON THREADS" HILARY BROWN

MAIN COURSE

*Pheasant Breast with Chanterelles and Grapes on
a Potato Cake*

Vegetable Purées

"THE PHEASANT WAS SPECTACULAR... THE NICEST I HAVE HAD
IN A LONG TIME" NED SHERRIN

DESSERT

Filo Gâteau with Exotic Fruits and Lavender Sabayon

Originally from New Zealand, Ross Burden now resides in Fulham. Ross took his zoology degree in New Zealand, while working part-time as a shark handler and trainer of dolphins. Currently he creates the cocktails at a trendy show-biz watering hole in London. At home Ross has an impressive stamp collection.

MUSSELS WITH SAFFRON IN A LIGHT BROTH

1.5 kg (3½ lb) mussels
90 ml (6 tbsp) olive oil
3 shallots, finely chopped
2 cloves garlic, finely chopped
10 ml (2 tsp) tomato purée
750 ml (1¼ pints) court bouillon
½ stem lemon grass, halved
2 bay leaves
50 g (2 oz) butter, chilled and diced
30 ml (2 tbsp) crème fraîche
15 ml (1 tbsp) each finely chopped tarragon,
  basil and chives
pinch of saffron threads
salt and freshly ground pepper
4 small red-skinned potatoes
1 courgette
1 aubergine
1 tomato, skinned and deseeded
few saffron threads, to garnish

Scrub the mussels thoroughly in cold water, removing the beards and discarding any open ones.

Heat 45 ml (3 tbsp) olive oil in a small saucepan over a low heat. Add the shallots and half of the garlic and cook gently until soft, about 5 minutes. Whisk in the tomato purée, then 500 ml (16 fl oz) court bouillon. Add the lemon grass and bay leaves and boil for 10 minutes. Remove and discard the lemon grass and bay leaves.

Whisk in the butter, a piece at a time, on and off the heat, making sure each piece is thoroughly incorporated before adding the next. Stir in the crème fraîche, herbs and saffron. Season with salt and pepper to taste. Keep warm.

Bring 250 ml (8 fl oz) court bouillon to the boil, with the remaining garlic added, in a large flameproof casserole or heavy-based pan. Add the mussels, cover tightly and steam over a medium heat for about 10 minutes until the mussels open; do not allow to boil dry. When cooked, remove the mussels from the pan with a slotted spoon, discarding any unopened ones.

Strain the cooking liquor through a muslin-lined sieve and add to the saffron broth. Remove the mussels from their shells.

Cut the potatoes and courgette into pieces about the size of a garlic clove. Cut the aubergine and tomato into 1 cm (½ inch) cubes. Heat a little olive oil in a pan and sauté each vegetable separately until tender. Drain on kitchen paper, season with salt and pepper and keep warm.

To serve, add the vegetables and mussels to the broth and ladle into warmed soup bowls. Garnish with a little saffron.

PHEASANT BREAST WITH CHANTERELLES AND GRAPES ON A POTATO PANCAKE

Use the carcasses from the pheasants to make a well-flavoured stock.

4 pheasant breasts
90 g (3½ oz) chanterelles or other wild
  mushrooms
150 g (5 oz) red grapes
salt and freshly ground black pepper
15 ml (1 tbsp) oil
40 g (1½ oz) butter, chilled and diced
85 ml (6 tbsp) white wine
300 ml (½ pint) pheasant stock

Potato Cakes:
350 g (12 oz) large potatoes
50 g (2 oz) clarified butter

To Serve:
chervil sprigs, to garnish
few drops of truffle oil (optional)

Trim the pheasant breasts. Clean the mushrooms thoroughly. Halve and deseed the grapes.

To make the potato cakes, peel and thinly slice the potatoes, then mix with the clarified butter. Season with salt and pepper. Form into 4 potato cakes, each 10 cm (4 inches) across and 5 mm (¼ inch) deep. Fry the potato cakes in a heavy-based pan, pressing down firmly, until crisp and golden brown on both sides; keep warm.

Heat 15 ml (1 tbsp) oil and 25 g (1 oz) butter in another pan, add the pheasant breasts and fry briefly over a high heat until well browned. Turn and repeat on the other side. The cooked pheasant breasts must remain pink inside otherwise they become dry. Using a slotted spoon, transfer to an ovenproof dish.

Add the mushrooms to the pan and sauté gently, adding the grapes when the mushrooms are almost cooked. Add to the pheasant and keep warm. Drain off the oil from the pan.

Deglaze the pan with the white wine. Reduce until almost completely evaporated, then add the stock. Boil rapidly to reduce until the sauce starts to thicken. Strain through a muslin-lined sieve into a clean pan and reheat.

Reheat the pheasant, mushrooms and grapes in a preheated oven at 220°C (425°F) mark 7 for 1 minute. Meanwhile whisk the remaining 15 g (½ oz) butter into the sauce, a piece at a time.

Place a potato cake on the centre of each warmed serving plate. Slice the pheasant and arrange on top of the potato cakes. Arrange the mushrooms, grapes and sprigs of chervil around the pheasant and moisten with the sauce. Sprinkle the pheasant with a drop of truffle oil to add richness to the dish, if desired. Serve immediately, accompanied by vegetable purées, such as carrot and potato, and parsnip purées.

FILO GÂTEAU WITH EXOTIC FRUITS AND LAVENDER SABAYON

1 packet of filo pastry
200 ml (⅓ pint) almond or olive oil
selection of tropical fruits, such as mango,
  star fruit, rambutan, passion fruit and
  miniature pineapple
25 ml (1½ tbsp) armagnac or brandy
5 ml (1 tsp) dried lavender
6 egg yolks
25 ml (1½ tbsp) sugar
45 ml (3 tbsp) freshly squeezed passion fruit
  juice, strained
icing sugar, for dredging

Cut twelve 10 cm (4 inch) circles from the filo pastry. Heat the oil in a deep frying pan and fry the filo circles, one at a time, over a moderately high heat until crisp and golden. Drain on kitchen paper.

Prepare the fruits as necessary and slice, reserving a little of each for decoration. Put the armagnac in a small bowl, sprinkle in the lavender and leave to macerate for a few minutes, then strain through a fine sieve.

Put the egg yolks, armagnac, sugar and strained passion fruit juice in a heavy-based pan and whisk vigorously over a very low heat. Continue whisking on and off the heat for about 7 minutes until the sabayon emulsifies and holds its creaminess.

Assemble the filo gâteaux on the serving plates: layer the filo circles in threes, with the sabayon and sliced tropical fruits, ending with a filo circle. Dredge with icing sugar and decorate with the reserved fruits.

REGIONAL HEATS
LONDON

ROSS BURDEN • MARWAN BADRAN • AMANDA DAWSON

MARWAN BADRAN'S MENU

STARTER

*Chicken Liver and Asparagus Terrine, served
with a Red Pepper Marmalade*

"THIS DISH LOOKS AS IF A LOT OF SKILL AND EFFORT HAS
GONE INTO IT" LOYD

MAIN COURSE

*Monkfish wrapped in Aubergine
Timbales of Rice and Broad Beans
Tomato and Tamarind Sauce*

"THIS IS VERY NICELY COOKED WITH AN UNUSUAL COMBINATION OF
AUBERGINES AND FISH" HILARY BROWN

DESSERT

*Halva and Rosewater Ice Cream, served with Quince
Syrup and Walnut Cake*

Marwan Badran lives in central London having emigrated from Iraq ten years ago. He has recently completed his five years as a medical student at the Middlesex hospital. Marwan is a serious collector of paintings and many of his friends are artists. He also enjoys playing bridge.

CHICKEN LIVER AND ASPARAGUS TERRINE

Serve this terrine with the Red Pepper Marmalade.

350 g (12 oz) chicken livers
150 ml (¼ pint) red wine
salt and freshly ground black pepper
10 savoy cabbage leaves (approximately)
450 g (1 lb) asparagus
2 large boneless chicken breasts, skinned
175 g (6 oz) belly pork
1 clove garlic, crushed
1 egg
5 ml (1 tsp) chopped thyme
15 ml (1 tbsp) fresh green peppercorns

Carefully trim the chicken livers and place in a shallow dish. Pour over the wine and leave to marinate for at least 1 hour. Drain and pat dry with kitchen paper. Season with salt and pepper.

Discard the hard stalks from the cabbage leaves. Blanch in boiling water until softened. Drain and pat dry with kitchen paper. Trim the tough stalks from the asparagus spears, then steam for about 5 minutes. Refresh in cold water, drain and set aside.

Roughly chop the chicken breasts; trim and roughly chop the belly pork. Place these in a food processor with the garlic and process until finely chopped. Add the egg, thyme and seasoning and work until evenly mixed. Turn into a bowl. Fold in the green peppercorns.

Butter a 23 x 7.5 cm (9 x 3 inch) terrine and line with the cabbage leaves, allowing them to overlap the sides so that they can be folded over the top after filling. Cover the base and sides of the lined terrine with two thirds of the chicken and pork mixture. Press two thirds of the asparagus spears onto the base and long sides of the terrine. Place the chicken livers along the middle of the terrine and cover with the remaining chicken mixture. Arrange the rest of the asparagus spears on top. Fold over the cabbage leaves to enclose the terrine.

Cover tightly with a double layer of foil, then place in a bain-marie or roasting tin containing enough hot water to come halfway up the sides of the terrine. Cook in a preheated oven at 180°C (350°F) mark 4 for 40 minutes. Allow to cool slightly before turning out and draining off any liquid. Serve warm, with the red pepper marmalade.

RED PEPPER MARMALADE

2 red peppers
1 onion
3 cloves garlic
60 ml (4 tbsp) red wine vinegar
30 ml (2 tbsp) demerara sugar
15 ml (1 tbsp) olive oil
salt and freshly ground black pepper

Halve, core and deseed the red peppers. Roughly chop the peppers, onion and garlic. Place in a small heavy-based pan with the remaining ingredients and simmer, covered, for about 1 hour, stirring from time to time, until nearly all the liquid has cooked off and the mixture is dense and shiny. Serve at room temperature.

MONKFISH WRAPPED IN AUBERGINE

675 g (1½ lb) monkfish, boned and trimmed
  of membrane
juice of 1 lime
5 ml (1 tsp) ground tropical peppercorns
  (see note)
2 aubergines
peanut oil, for frying
salt

Cut the fish into 12 equal pieces and place in a shallow dish. Sprinkle with the lime juice and ground peppercorns and leave to marinate for 1 hour.

Cut the aubergines lengthwise into wafer-thin slices. Heat a thin layer of oil in a frying pan and fry the aubergine slices in batches until softened. Drain on kitchen paper.

Drain the fish and wrap each piece in a slice of aubergine. Season with a little salt. Bake uncovered in a preheated oven at 220°C (425°F) mark 7 for 5 minutes. Serve immediately, with the rice and broad bean timbales, and the tomato and tamarind sauce.

Note: 'Tropical peppercorns' are mixed coloured peppercorns including black, pink and green ones – sold in tubs. They are available from delicatessens and most larger supermarkets.

TIMBALES OF RICE AND BROAD BEANS

225 g (8 oz) long-grain rice
salt and freshly ground black pepper
225 g (8 oz) shelled fresh or frozen broad
  beans
30 ml (2 tbsp) peanut oil
handful of chopped dill

Rinse the rice in cold water, then cook in boiling salted water until just tender; drain thoroughly.

If using fresh broad beans blanch briefly in boiling water to loosen the skins; drain and peel off the skins. If using frozen ones, simply allow to defrost, then the skins should slip off easily.

Heat the oil in a heavy-based frying pan, add the rice, broad beans and half of the dill and fry gently for 2-3 minutes, stirring all the time. Gently stir in the rest of the dill and season with salt and pepper to taste.

Press the rice mixture into 4 warmed individual moulds or ramekins, then carefully turn out onto hot serving plates.

TOMATO AND TAMARIND SAUCE

450 g (1 lb) onions
450 g (1 lb) tomatoes
4 cloves garlic
50 g (2 oz) block of tamarind
30 ml (2 tbsp) peanut oil
5 ml (1 tsp) ground tropical peppercorns
600 ml (1 pint) well-flavoured fish stock
salt (if necessary)

Roughly chop the onions, tomatoes and garlic. Chop the tamarind, place in a small bowl and pour on boiling water to cover. Leave to soften for 5 minutes, then mash the tamarind with the water to a thick pulp.

Heat the oil in a saucepan, add the onions and soften until transparent. Add all the other ingredients, adding salt only if necessary. Bring to the boil, lower the heat, cover and simmer for 30 minutes.

Press the sauce through a fine sieve and return to the cleaned pan. Reduce by fast boiling to 300 ml (½ pint).

HALVA AND ROSEWATER ICE CREAM

The Quince Syrup (below) and Walnut Cake (right) complement this ice cream perfectly.

3 large eggs
50 g (2 oz) caster sugar
5 ml (1 tsp) rosewater
300 ml (½ pint) whipping cream
100 g (4 oz) halva

In a bowl, whisk the eggs, sugar and rosewater together until the mixture is pale and thick enough to leave a ribbon trail when the whisk is lifted.

In another bowl, whip the cream until it forms soft peaks, then crumble in the halva. Lightly fold into the whisked egg mixture.

Turn into a freezerproof container and freeze until firm. Remove from the freezer for a few minutes before serving and leave to soften at room temperature.

Serve the ice cream on a pool of quince syrup, surrounded by thin slices of walnut cake.

QUINCE SYRUP

50 g (2 oz) caster sugar
1 quince, peeled and chopped
2 green cardamoms

Dissolve the sugar in 900 ml (1½ pints) water in a heavy-based pan over a low heat. Bring to the boil and simmer for 15 minutes. Add the quince and carda-moms and simmer, uncovered, for approximately 1½ hours or until the syrup turns a rich amber colour. Press through a sieve, discarding the fruit. If the syrup is too thin, reduce by boiling to about 200 ml (7 fl oz). Cool before serving.

WALNUT CAKE

50 g (2 oz) unsalted butter, softened
100 g (4 oz) walnuts, finely chopped
5 ml (1 tsp) baking powder
15 ml (1 tbsp) plain flour
100 g (4 oz) caster sugar
1 egg white, size 3
2 egg whites, size 4

Butter an 18 cm (7 inch) springform cake tin and line the base with greaseproof paper.

In a bowl, beat the butter with the chopped walnuts, baking powder, flour and 75 g (3 oz) of the sugar until evenly mixed. Add the size 3 egg white and mix again.

In another bowl, whisk the two size 4 egg whites until stiff, then gradually sprinkle in the remaining 25 g (1 oz) sugar, whisking the time. Carefully fold the two mixtures together and spoon into the prepared tin. Level the surface.

Bake in a preheated oven at 180°C (350°F) mark 4 for 20 minutes or until a knife inserted in the middle of the cake comes out clean. Allow to cool a little before releasing the cake from the tin. Serve warm or cool.

REGIONAL HEATS

LONDON

ROSS BURDEN • MARWAN BADRAN • AMANDA DAWSON

AMANDA DAWSON'S MENU

STARTER

*Raw Salmon and Scallops in a Citrus Marinade, served with a
Courgette and Basil Gâteau*

"A PERFECT FIRST COURSE... I LOVE THE CRUNCHINESS AND THE CONTRAST
OF THE SHARPNESS WITH THE OIL" LOYD

MAIN COURSE

*Roasted Breast of Wood Pigeon with Forest Mushrooms
and a Balsamic Vinegar and Port Sauce
Puy Lentils*

DESSERT

*Trio of Hot and Cold Orange Desserts spiked with
Scotch Whisky*

A manda Dawson from Fulham is an articled clerk to a firm of solicitors in the city. For the past two years Amanda has narrowly missed a place in the regional finals and we are delighted that she has been successful this year. Amanda is an enthusiastic squash player and enjoys playing the cello.

RAW SALMON AND SCALLOPS IN A CITRUS MARINADE

This delicate marinated fish starter is served with Courgette and Basil Gâteau (right).

400 g (14 oz) very fresh salmon
2 large king scallops, cleaned (about 125 g (4 oz) scallop meat)
7 g (¼ oz) butter

Marinade:
finely grated rind and juice of ½ lemon
finely grated rind of ½ lime
juice of 1 lime
25 g (1 oz) parsley, finely chopped
15 g (½ oz) basil, finely chopped
5 ml (1 tsp) mixed coloured peppercorns (pink, green, black and white), finely crushed
pinch of salt, to taste
120 ml (4 fl oz) olive oil (preferably extra-virgin)

Cut the salmon into wafer-thin slices. Separate the scallop corals and set aside. Slice the white scallop meat into wafer-thin discs. Arrange the salmon and white scallop discs on 4 individual serving plates.

Blanch the grated lemon and lime rinds in boiling water for 1 minute; drain in a fine sieve. Mix together with all of the other ingredients for the marinade and stir well. Pour evenly over the fish and leave to marinate for 5 minutes.

Meanwhile heat the butter in a very small pan and sauté the scallop corals over a very high heat for about 5 seconds. Remove from the pan and slice each coral in half lengthwise.

Place a courgette gâteau in the centre of the marinated fish and top with a warm halved scallop coral.

COURGETTE AND BASIL GÂTEAUX

6 medium courgettes, about 875 g (1¾ lb)
4 cloves garlic
15 ml (1 tbsp) olive oil
15 g (½ oz) basil leaves, roughly torn
2.5 ml (½ tsp) curry powder
2 egg yolks, size 1
salt and freshly ground black pepper
basil leaves, to garnish

Chop the courgettes very finely and place in a large saucepan with the whole garlic cloves and oil. Cover and sweat over a low heat until the courgettes are well cooked. Drain thoroughly in a sieve, pressing to remove as much moisture as possible. Discard the garlic.

Put the courgettes, basil, curry powder, egg yolks and seasoning into a food processor and process until smooth.

Lightly oil 4 dariole moulds with olive oil and divide the courgette mixture between them. Cover the moulds tightly and steam over a pan of boiling water for 6 minutes. Alternatively cook in a bain-marie (saucepan containing enough hot water to come halfway up the sides of the moulds). Allow to cool, then place in the refrigerator for 2-3 hours until well chilled.

Turn the chilled firm gâteaux out on to serving plates and garnish with basil to serve.

ROASTED BREAST OF WOOD PIGEON WITH FOREST MUSHROOMS AND A BALSAMIC VINEGAR AND PORT SAUCE

For this recipe, choose plump wood pigeons. Carefully remove the whole breasts and use the rest of the carcasses to make the stock. You will need to marinate the pigeon (and soak the mushrooms) overnight.

3 plump wood pigeons' breasts
20 ml (4 tsp) walnut oil
20 ml (4 tsp) hazelnut oil
10 ml (2 tsp) olive oil
50 g (2 oz) mixed dried forest mushrooms
    (chanterelles, horn of plenty, ceps)
40 g (1½ oz) butter
1 small onion
10 ml (2 tsp) dried herbs de Provence
60 ml (2 fl oz) balsamic vinegar
175 ml (6 fl oz) port
300 ml (½ pint) game stock
salt and freshly ground black pepper
few fresh chanterelles (if available)

Remove the skin from the pigeon breasts and prick the flesh lightly all over with a fork. Place in a shallow dish and drizzle with 10 ml (2 tsp) each of walnut, hazelnut and olive oil. Turn the pigeon breasts to coat with the oils, cover and leave to marinate in a cool place overnight.

Meanwhile put the dried mushrooms in a small bowl, add cold water to cover and leave to soak overnight.

Melt 15 g (½ oz) of the butter in a frying pan and seal the pigeon breasts over a very high heat for 1 minute each side. Transfer to a baking tray and cover with foil.

To make the sauce, chop the onion very finely. Heat 10 ml (2 tsp) each of hazelnut and walnut oil with 15 g (½ oz) butter in a pan.

Add the onion and cook for 2 minutes until softened. Drain the soaked mushrooms, reserving the liquid, and add to the pan with the herbs. Fry, stirring, for 5 minutes.

Add the vinegar to the pan and boil vigorously until the mixture is almost dry. Add the port and boil to reduce by half. Add the stock and reserved mushroom liquor, and reduce by one third. Season with salt and pepper to taste; keep warm.

Cook the pigeon breasts in a preheated oven at 220°C (425°F) mark 7 for 5 minutes. Remove from the oven and leave to rest covered with foil for 5 minutes. Meanwhile sauté the fresh mushrooms in a little butter until tender.

To serve, thinly slice the pigeon breasts and arrange on warmed serving plates on a pile of lentils. Garnish with the sautéed chanterelles and surround with the sauce.

PUY LENTILS

175 g (6 oz) puy lentils
1 onion, chopped
10 ml (2 tsp) dried herbs de Provence
salt and freshly ground black pepper

Put the lentils in a saucepan, add cold water to cover and bring to the boil. Boil rapidly for 5 minutes, then drain and refresh in cold water; drain again.

Put the lentils, onion, herbs and salt and pepper into a large saucepan. Cover with cold water and bring to the boil. Cook until the lentils are tender but not mushy and the water is absorbed – add more water during cooking if necessary.

Note: The lentils may take anything from 25-40 minutes to cook depending on their type and age, but once cooked they can be kept warm over a low heat or reheated.

WHISKY AND ORANGE BRIOCHE PUDDING

For this pudding you will need some of the Whisky and Orange Syrup (see overleaf).

75 g (3 oz) brioche crumbs
50 g (2 oz) amaretti biscuits, crushed
5 ml (1 tsp) ground cinnamon
10 ml (2 tsp) caster sugar
150 ml (¼ pint) full-fat milk
150 ml (¼ pint) whipping cream
60 ml (2 fl oz) Whisky and Orange Syrup
  (see overleaf), cooled
1½ eggs, size 2, beaten

Brush 4 ramekins with melted butter and dust with caster sugar. In a bowl, mix the brioche and amaretti crumbs together with the cinnamon and sugar.

In another bowl, mix together the milk, cream, syrup and eggs until evenly blended. Lightly fold in the crumb mixture. Divide evenly between the ramekins and bake in a preheated oven at 180°C (350°F) mark 4 for 50 minutes until risen and golden.

To serve, place a ramekin on each plate. Arrange a portion of whisky and orange ice cream, a cinnamon brioche toast and a spoonful of grapes in syrup on the plate. Serve immediately, while the pudding is still warm.

WHISKY AND ORANGE ICE CREAM

Prepare the Whisky and Orange Syrup (see right) in advance, as you will need to add some to the ice cream.

150 ml (¼ pint) full-fat milk
1 egg, size 2
20 ml (4 tsp) caster sugar
150 ml (¼ pint) whipping cream
45 ml (3 tbsp) Whisky and Orange Syrup
  (see right)

Cinnamon Brioche Toasts:
4 slices brioche, about 1 cm (½ inch) thick
melted butter, for brushing
ground cinnamon, for sprinkling
icing sugar, for sprinkling

Heat the milk in a small pan, until almost but not quite boiling. Beat the egg and sugar together in a bowl. Pour on the warm milk, stirring constantly. Return to the pan and stir continuously over a low heat until the mixture is thick enough to coat the back of the wooden spoon. Leave to cool, then stir in the cream and syrup.

Freeze the mixture in an ice cream machine for 20 minutes. Alternatively, if you do not have an ice cream machine, pour into a shallow freezerproof container and freeze for about 3 hours until firm, whisking 2 or 3 times during freezing to break down the ice crystals.

To prepare the brioche toasts, brush both sides of the brioche slices with melted butter and sprinkle with cinnamon and icing sugar. Toast under a hot grill until crisp and lightly browned. Serve with the ice cream.

GRAPES IN WHISKY AND ORANGE SYRUP

7 oranges
30 ml (2 tbsp) caster sugar
30 ml (2 tbsp) marmalade
60 ml (2 fl oz) whisky

To Serve:
24 seedless green grapes

Finely pare the rind from the oranges using a zester and put into a saucepan. Add boiling water to cover and simmer for 3 minutes. Drain and refresh under cold water.

Squeeze the juice from the oranges and place in a saucepan with the rind, sugar and two thirds of the marmalade. Bring to the boil and boil steadily to reduce by half. Add the whisky and boil for 2 minutes.

At this stage strain 45 ml (3 tbsp) of the syrup and set aside for the ice cream.

Add the remaining marmalade to the syrup and warm slightly to melt the marmalade; do not boil. Allow to cool. Strain the requisite amount of syrup and set aside for the Brioche Pudding.

To serve, remove about two thirds of the rind with a slotted spoon, then add the grapes to the remaining syrup.

REGIONAL HEATS
WALES

KERRY CHURCH • PATTI HALL • ROBIN MACHIN

WINNER

KERRY CHURCH'S MENU

STARTER

Warm Salad of Red Mullet with a Lemon Balm Dressing

MAIN COURSE

Noisettes of Welsh Lamb

Fresh Herb Pasta

Tomato Sauce with Sun-dried Tomatoes

"BOTH THE LAMB AND PASTA ARE DELICIOUS" DAVID BURKE

DESSERT

Pan-fried Pears with a Blackberry Coulis, Almond Biscuits

and Amaretto Cream

"I RELISHED THAT. IT WAS DELICIOUS" JOAN BAKEWELL

Kerry lives in Cardiff and works as a troubleshooter in a clinical diagnostics laboratory, where research into diseases such as hepatitis is carried out. Water-colour painting is an important relaxation, and Kerry's subjects include many of the unusual buildings which surround the city of Cardiff. Her more energetic pursuits include mountain biking with her children, Martin and Jenny, who are also great cooks.

WARM SALAD OF RED MULLET WITH A LEMON BALM DRESSING

In your selection of salad leaves, include some with 'bite'; for example radicchio, watercress and frisée.

2 red mullet, each about 225 g (8 oz)
4 lemon balm sprigs
60 ml (4 tbsp) dry white wine

Dressing:
½ small onion, finely chopped
60 ml (4 tbsp) white wine vinegar
60 ml (4 tbsp) grapeseed oil
90 ml (6 tbsp) dry white wine
15 ml (1 tbsp) chopped lemon balm leaves
salt and freshly ground black pepper

To Serve:
assorted salad leaves

Thoroughly clean the mullet and place on a piece of lightly oiled foil. Put a sprig of lemon balm inside each fish and fold up the sides of the foil. Pour on the white wine, add the other 2 lemon balm sprigs and fold over the foil to form a loose parcel.

Place the parcel on a baking sheet. Cook in a preheated oven at 190°C (375°F) mark 5 for about 20 minutes, depending on the size of the fish, until tender. After cooking, strain off the liquid from the parcel and reserve for the dressing. Remove the bones from the fish; divide the flesh into flakes.

To make the dressing, put the onion, vinegar, oil, wine and the reserved liquid in a small saucepan. Bring to the boil and boil to reduce by about one third; keep hot.

Tear the salad leaves into manageable-sized pieces. Arrange the salad leaves and the flaked mullet on individual plates. Add the chopped lemon balm to the hot dressing and season with salt and pepper to taste. Pour the dressing over the salad and serve immediately.

NOISETTES OF WELSH LAMB

4 large noisettes of lamb, each about
  150 g (5 oz)
25 g (1 oz) butter, melted
75 g (3 oz) fresh breadcrumbs
15 ml (1 tbsp) finely chopped rosemary
salt and freshly ground black pepper
a little beaten egg yolk

Trim the chops of excess fat if necessary. Combine the melted butter, breadcrumbs and rosemary in a bowl and season with salt and pepper to taste. Coat the lamb on both sides with a very thin layer of beaten egg and cover liberally with the crumb mixture.

Place the noisettes in an ovenproof dish and cook in a preheated oven at 220°C (425°F) mark 7 for 20-25 minutes, depending on the thickness of the noisettes, until tender. Serve immediately, with fresh herb pasta.

FRESH HERB PASTA

15 g (½ oz) parsley sprigs
175 g (6 oz) strong plain flour
2 eggs, size 2

Blanch the parsley sprigs in boiling water for 2 minutes, drain and pat dry on kitchen paper, then chop finely.

Place the flour, eggs and chopped parsley in a bowl and stir together using a fork, then work the mixture with your hands to form a dough. Turn out and knead on a lightly floured surface for 3-4 minutes until smooth. Wrap in cling film and set aside in a cool place for at least 30 minutes before rolling out.

If using a pasta machine, put the dough through the tagliatelle setting. Alternatively roll out thinly on a lightly floured surface to a large rectangle. Allow to dry out slightly, then cut into 1 cm (¾ inch) wide strips for tagliatelle.

Cook the pasta in plenty of boiling salted water for about 3 minutes until *al dente* (tender but still firm to the bite). Drain and serve with the tomato sauce.

TOMATO SAUCE WITH SUN-DRIED TOMATOES

Flavourful Italian plum tomatoes are the best ones to choose for this sauce. Use the oil from the sun-dried tomato jar or extra-virgin olive oil for frying.

4 tomatoes
25 ml (1½ tbsp) oil
2 cloves garlic, finely chopped
6 sun-dried tomatoes in oil, drained and
  chopped
75 ml (5 tbsp) white wine
15 ml (1 tbsp) chopped basil leaves

To skin the tomatoes, immerse in boiling water for about 30 seconds, or hold on a fork over a gas flame for 15-30 seconds turning as the skin blisters, then peel away the skins.

Heat the oil in a saucepan, add the chopped garlic and fry gently for 2-3 minutes. Chop the tomatoes and add to the saucepan together with the sun-dried tomatoes and wine. Simmer for about 15 minutes, stirring occasionally. Add the chopped basil just before serving.

PAN-FRIED PEARS WITH A BLACKBERRY COULIS, ALMOND BISCUITS AND AMARETTO CREAM

4 ripe pears
25 g (1 oz) unsalted butter

Almond Biscuits:

2 egg whites
100 g (3½ oz) ground almonds
75 g (3 oz) caster sugar
12 flaked almonds

Blackberry Coulis:

150 g (5 oz) blackberries
juice of ½ lemon
25 g (1 oz) icing sugar

Amaretto Cream:

150 ml (¼ pint) double cream
30 ml (2 tbsp) Amaretto di Saronno liqueur
5 ml (1 tsp) icing sugar

To Decorate:

lemon rind shreds, blanched

To make the almond biscuits, in a bowl, whisk the egg whites until stiff but not dry, then fold in the ground almonds and sugar. Transfer the mixture to a piping bag fitted with a large plain nozzle and pipe 12 small and 4 larger biscuits on to a baking sheet lined with non-stick baking parchment. Press a flaked almond on the top of each of the smaller biscuits. Cook in a preheated oven at 190°C (375°F) mark 5 for 15 minutes. Transfer to a wire rack to cool.

To make the blackberry coulis, purée the blackberries in a food processor or blender until smooth, then pass through a sieve to remove the seeds. Add the lemon juice and icing sugar and stir well to dissolve the icing sugar.

To prepare the amaretto cream, whip the cream until thick, then fold in the liqueur and icing sugar.

Peel the pears, cut lengthwise into 3 equal pieces and remove the cores. Melt the butter in a large deep frying pan, add the pears and fry for about 5 minutes, turning frequently to ensure they are browned on all sides; keep warm.

To assemble the dessert, spoon the blackberry coulis on to individual serving plates. Cover the larger biscuits with amaretto cream and place one in the middle of each plate. Arrange the pears in a radial pattern around the biscuit. Place the smaller biscuits between the pears, decorate with thin strips of lemon rind and serve immediately.

REGIONAL HEATS

WALES

KERRY CHURCH • PATTI HALL • ROBIN MACHIN

PATTI HALL'S MENU

STARTER

Stuffed Pears with Poppy Seed 'Cream'

"THIS MENU HAS GREAT BEAUTY TO IT – YOU COULD
ALMOST FRAME IT" JOAN BAKEWELL

MAIN COURSE

Fillet of Welsh Lamb with an Elderberry and Orange Sauce

Spiced Creamed Potatoes

Buttered Leeks with Tarragon

Carrot Batons

DESSERT

Amaretti Chocolate Tortes

"THIS IS WHAT A CHOCOLATE DESSERT SHOULD BE" DAVID BURKE

Patti emigrated to Cardiff twelve years ago from Yorkshire. She is a component buyer for a nearby electronics firm specialising in circuit boards. In her spare time Patti is the lead singer with a local pop group. By way of contrast, she also referees the local five-a-side football team.

Stuffed Pears with Poppy Seed 'Cream'

2 large ripe, firm dessert pears
30 ml (2 tbsp) lemon juice
50-75 g (2-3 oz) blue Stilton cheese
50 g (2 oz) low-fat soft cheese
10 ml (2 tsp) finely chopped celery
10 ml (2 tsp) finely chopped walnuts
30 ml (2 tbsp) fromage frais
30-45 ml (2-3 tbsp) single cream
5-10 ml (1-2 tsp) poppy seeds
salt and freshly ground black pepper

Carefully remove the cores from the pears using an apple corer or teaspoon and immediately brush the cavities with lemon juice. Crumble the Stilton into a bowl, add the soft cheese, celery and walnuts and mix to a stiff paste. Fill the pear cavities with the cheese mixture, pressing it in as firmly as possible. Cover and chill in the refrigerator until ready to serve.

To make the dressing, whisk together the fromage frais, single cream, remaining lemon juice and poppy seeds. Season with salt and pepper to taste. Thin the dressing with a little extra cream, if desired.

To serve, spoon a little of the dressing onto each serving plate. Cut each pear in half lengthways, then slice, fan out and arrange cut-side down on the dressing. Serve immediately.

Fillet of Welsh Lamb with an Elderberry and Orange Sauce

450-700 g (1-1½ lb) loin fillet of lamb, in one piece
3 oranges
10 ml (2 tsp) galangal mixed with 15 ml (1 tbsp) hot water
salt and freshly ground black pepper
25 g (1 oz) granulated sugar
150 ml (¼ pint) elderberry syrup
15 ml (1 tbsp) balsamic vinegar

Trim the fillet of lamb and tie into a neat shape with cotton string. Grate the rind and squeeze the juice from two of the oranges; mix with the galangal and hot water. Place the meat in a dish, pour over the orange mixture, cover and leave to marinate in a cool place for several hours or overnight, turning occasionally.

Lift the meat out of the bowl, drain and pat dry with kitchen paper. Strain the marinade and reserve. Season the meat with salt and pepper and place in a roasting tin. Bake in a preheated oven at 200°C (400°F) mark 6 for 30 minutes.

Finely pare the rind from the remaining orange and cut into small julienne strips. Dissolve the sugar in 150 ml (¼ pint) water in a pan over a low heat. Add the orange rind, bring to the boil and simmer for 5-10 minutes. Drain and set aside to cool.

When the lamb is almost cooked, mix together the reserved marinade, juice of the remaining orange, the elderberry syrup and balsamic vinegar in a small pan. Slowly bring to the boil.

Remove the lamb from the roasting tin, wrap in foil and leave to rest in a warm place. Add the lamb juices to the marinade mixture and simmer until slightly reduced; check the seasoning. Unwrap the lamb and cut into 2 cm (¾ inch) thick slices.

To serve, spoon a little of the sauce onto each plate and arrange the lamb in overlapping slices on top. Drizzle a little sauce over the meat and garnish with the orange rind julienne. Serve immediately, with the accompaniments.

Note: Galangal is a root that resembles ginger. It is available from oriental food stores.

SPICED CREAMED POTATOES

450 g (1 lb) potatoes
salt and freshly ground black pepper
15 g (½ oz) butter
30 ml (2 tbsp) single cream
2.5 ml (½ tsp) ground coriander
2.5 ml (½ oz) freshly grated nutmeg
pinch of ground cumin

Cook the potatoes in boiling salted water until tender; drain thoroughly. Mash with a potato masher, then pass through a sieve into a bowl. Beat in the butter and single cream. Add the spices and pepper to taste. Beat well and reheat if necessary before serving.

BUTTERED LEEKS WITH TARRAGON

450 g (1 lb) young leeks
50-75 g (2-3 oz) butter
1 large bunch of tarragon
salt and freshly ground black pepper

Trim the leeks and cut into 7.5 cm (3 inch) lengths. Cut each piece lengthways into 4 slices and wash thoroughly. Drain and pat dry with kitchen paper. Tie half of the tarragon into a bunch with cotton string.

Melt the butter in a saucepan. Add the leeks and tarragon bunch to the pan and stir well. Cover and cook over a low heat, shaking the pan occasionally, for 10 minutes or until the leeks are tender but still retain their colour. Meanwhile, strip the remaining tarragon leaves from their stalks and chop finery.

Just before serving, discard the bunch of tarragon. Add the chopped tarragon to the leeks, stir and season with salt and pepper to taste. Serve immediately.

AMARETTI CHOCOLATE TORTES

4 amaretti biscuits
250 g (9 oz) plain dark chocolate
30 ml (2 tbsp) liquid glucose or glycerine
30 ml (2 tbsp) Amaretto di Saronno liqueur
300 ml (½ pint) double cream
12-16 blanched almonds
150 ml (¼ pint) single cream
knob of butter

Line the bases of 4 ramekin dishes with circles of greaseproof paper. Crush the amaretti biscuits finely and divide evenly between the ramekins.

Break 8 oz (225 g) of the chocolate into small pieces and put into a heatproof bowl with the liquid glucose or glycerine and liqueur. Place the bowl over a saucepan of hot water until the chocolate is melted and smooth. Remove the bowl from the pan and leave to cool slightly.

Whip the double cream until just thickened, then stir 30 ml (2 tbsp) into the chocolate mixture. Add this chocolate mixture to the remaining cream and stir until well blended. Pour the mixture into the ramekins, dividing it evenly, and tap the ramekins to level the surface of the mixture. Chill in the refrigerator for at least 45 minutes to set firmly.

Meanwhile melt the remaining chocolate. Dip each almond into the chocolate to half coat, and place on a foil-lined plate to set. Reserve the remaining chocolate.

To serve, re-melt the reserved chocolate and stir in the butter. Spoon into a small greaseproof paper piping bag fitted with a very fine plain nozzle. Run a knife around each ramekin. Place an inverted plate centrally over each ramekin and invert the dish and plate. Carefully remove the ramekins and greaseproof paper. Pour a little cream around each torte, pipe lines of chocolate on the cream and feather with the point of a skewer. Decorate the tortes with the half-coated almonds.

REGIONAL HEATS

WALES

KERRY CHURCH • PATTI HALL • ROBIN MACHIN

ROBIN MACHIN'S MENU

STARTER

Spicy Fish Soup

MAIN COURSE

Barbary Duck Breast with Honey and Thyme

Seasonal Vegetables

"THIS IS A GOOD HONEST DISH THAT IS ASSERTIVE ENOUGH TO
FOLLOW THE SOUP" LOYD

DESSERT

Mango Brulée

"I THOUGHT THE CRUST WAS EXCELLENT... THAT WAS A
PROPER BRULÉE CRUST" DAVID BURKE

Formerly a paratrooper, Robin has settled for a somewhat quieter life in Creigiau, not far from Cardiff. He now works in the competitive field of computer software sales. As a leisure activity he enjoys a spot of archery. Robin is also currently learning the fascinating science of Reflexology.

SPICY FISH SOUP

A flavoursome fish stock is essential for this soup. I buy a large bag of assorted fish bones from my local fish market. It is important to clean the fish bones thoroughly and trim off any dark skin to ensure the stock is a good colour. You will need a very large pan – an old preserving pan is ideal.

Fish Stock:
½ onion, chopped
3 cloves garlic, finely chopped
2 thin green chillies, chopped
50 g (2 oz) chorizos or other smoked
  sausages, sliced
about 1 kg (2 lb) trimmed fish bones (plaice,
  halibut etc)
225 g (8 oz) spider crab legs
1 bay leaf
salt and freshly ground black pepper

Soup:
finely pared strip of lemon rind, thinly
  shredded
50 g (2 oz) raw prawns, shelled
50 g (2 oz) raw cockles, shelled
1 small cuttlefish or squid (optional), cut
  into strips
5 ml (1 tsp) chopped parsley
8 mussels, cleaned
8 clams, cleaned
4 Queen scallops, cleaned (coral reserved)
4 raw king prawns
50 g (2 oz) mushrooms, thinly sliced
2 spring onions (white part only), chopped
5 ml (1 tsp) chopped dill

In a very large deep heavy-based pan, fry the chopped onion, garlic, chillies and smoked sausage slices for 5 minutes, stirring frequently. Add 2 litres (3½ pints) boiling water, the fish bones, spider crab legs, bay leaf and seasoning. Cover and simmer for 20 minutes, skimming occasionally. Uncover and boil to reduce to about 1 litre (1¾ pints).

Strain the stock into the base of a steamer pan and add the shredded lemon rind, shelled prawns, cockles, cuttlefish if using, and parsley. Bring to the boil.

Place the mussels, clams, white scallop meat and king prawns in the top of the steamer, cover and steam for approximately 4 minutes.

Transfer a ladleful of the hot stock to a small pan, add the scallop coral and squid if using and poach gently for about 30 seconds until cooked.

To serve, divide the mushroom slices and spring onions between warmed soup bowls. Pour in the soup and add the steamed fish. Add the scallop coral and squid if using and sprinkle with chopped dill to serve.

Note: If possible use almond clams for this soup; make sure you remove the tough white muscle as you prepare them.

BARBARY DUCK BREAST WITH HONEY AND THYME

30 ml (2 tbsp) oil or butter
4 Barbary duck breasts
4 shallots, diced
juice of 1 lemon
10 ml (2 tsp) chopped thyme
30 ml (2 tbsp) clear honey
10 ml (2 tsp) soy sauce
finely pared rind of ½ lemon, thinly sliced

Heat the oil or butter in a large heavy-based frying pan, add the duck breasts skin-side down and fry over a moderate heat for 6-8 minutes. Turn the duck breasts over, lower the heat and cook until almost tender.

Add the shallots, lemon juice and thyme. Bring to the boil, add the honey and soy sauce and cook for 2 minutes.

Remove the duck breasts and strain off the fat from the pan. Add the lemon rind shreds to the juices remaining in the pan and bring back to the boil. Meanwhile slice the duck breasts and arrange on individual plates. Pour the pan juices and lemon rind over the duck and serve immediately, with seasonal vegetables.

MANGO BRULÉE

1 ripe mango
600 ml (1 pint) double cream
3 drops of vanilla essence
2 eggs
2 egg yolks
30 ml (2 tbsp) caster sugar

Topping:
60 ml (4 tbsp) demerara sugar

Peel the mango and cut into slices, discarding the stone. Arrange the mango slices in the bases of 4 ramekins.

Pour the cream into a glass jug, add the vanilla essence and warm in the microwave. (Alternatively warm the cream mixture in a heavy-based pan over a low heat.) In a bowl, beat together the eggs, egg yolks and caster sugar. Pour on the warmed cream and blend well.

Pour the mixture into the ramekins and place in a bain-marie (or a roasting tin containing enough water to come half-way up the sides of the ramekins). Bake in a preheated oven at 190°C (375°F) mark 5 for 30-40 minutes. Allow to cool.

When cool sprinkle each one with 15 ml (1 tbsp) demerara sugar and place under a hot grill for 2-3 minutes until the topping caramelises. Leave to stand for about 5 minutes before serving.

REGIONAL HEATS

THE EAST

RICHARD KUCH • SHIRLEY FAULKNER • HUW WILLIAMS

WINNER

RICHARD KUCH'S MENU

STARTER

*Rubannes of Turbot with Pink Grapefruit, served
with a Vermouth Sauce*

MAIN COURSE

*Stuffed Pork Tenderloin with a Rosemary and Garlic Crust,
served with a Madeira Sauce*
Carrot and Leek Timbales

"COOKING PORK WITH ROSEMARY IS UNUSUAL BUT I THOUGHT
IT WAS VERY NICE" HANNAH GORDON

DESSERT

*Sablés of Caramelised Apple Rings, served with a
Blackcurrant Coulis*

Richard Kuch comes from Stamford in Lincolnshire. About ten years ago he converted an old post office into his hairdressing salon, where he has been responsible for many prize-winning creations. He has also won prizes for his allotment, where he not only grows vegetables but has constructed a beautiful garden. For relaxing evenings, Richard has taught himself the intricate craft of lace-making.

RUBANNES OF TURBOT WITH PINK GRAPEFRUIT, SERVED WITH A VERMOUTH SAUCE

200 g (7 oz) skinless salmon fillet
1 egg white (unbeaten)
300 ml (½ pint) double cream
1 bunch of chives, finely chopped
salt
1 pink grapefruit
10 ml (2 tsp) sugar
3 dashes of Grenadine
16 young spinach leaves
450 g (1 lb) skinless turbot fillet

Sauce:
150 g (5 oz) butter, chilled
2 shallots, finely chopped
90 ml (6 tbsp) Noilly Prat
90 ml (6 tbsp) fish stock
300 ml (½ pint) double cream

To Garnish:
chopped chives

Cut the salmon into small pieces and work in a food processor until smooth, then pass through a fine sieve into a bowl. Place the bowl over ice, add the egg white and mix to a smooth paste. Add the cream slowly, beating constantly, then add the chives and salt to taste. Mix thoroughly, cover and place in the refrigerator.

Finely pare the rind from the grapefruit and cut into fine julienne strips. Blanch the julienne strips in boiling water for 1 minute, drain and refresh with cold water, then place in a small heavy-based saucepan with the sugar and just enough water to cover. Stir over a low heat until the sugar has dissolved. Continue stirring until the sugar has just caramelised, then carefully add the grenadine. Stir until almost caramelised, then remove from the heat. Drain the grapefruit rind julienne and reserve.

Peel and segment the grapefruit over a bowl to catch the juice, discarding all white pith. Reserve the juice for the sauce.

Butter 4 ramekins. Blanch the spinach leaves in boiling water for a few seconds, drain then refresh with cold water; drain thoroughly.

Slice the turbot diagonally, then cut 12 circles to fit the bases of the ramekins. Trim the spinach leaves to the same size. Place a circle of turbot in each ramekin. Cover with a layer of salmon mousse, then two trimmed spinach leaves. Add another circle of turbot and two more spinach leaves. Cover with the rest of the salmon mousse and finally top with a circle of turbot.

Cover the ramekins with buttered greaseproof paper. Place in a bain-marie (or roasting tin containing enough hot water to come halfway up the sides of the ramekins). Bake in a preheated oven at 180°C (350°F) mark 4 for 15-20 minutes, until cooked through.

Meanwhile, make the sauce. Melt 25 g (1 oz) of the butter in a saucepan, add the shallots and sweat until softened, then add the Noilly Prat and fish stock. Reduce by half, then add the reserved grapefruit juice and reduce slightly. Add the cream and reduce by half. Cut the remaining butter into small pieces and whisk into the sauce, one piece at a time.

To serve, turn the "rubannes" out on to warmed serving plates. Pour over some of the sauce and garnish with chives. Arrange some grapefruit segments on each plate and garnish with the caramelised grapefruit rind. Serve the remaining sauce separately.

STUFFED PORK TENDERLOIN WITH A ROSEMARY AND GARLIC CRUST, SERVED WITH A MADEIRA SAUCE

900 g (2 lb) pork tenderloin (fillet)
12 fresh dates, stoned

Crust:
1 small bunch of rosemary
3 cloves garlic, chopped
50 g (2 oz) breadcrumbs
5 ml (1 tsp) salt
2.5 ml (½ tsp) freshly ground black pepper
50 g (2 oz) butter, melted

Sauce:
100 g (3½ oz) butter
1 onion, chopped
50 ml (3½ tbsp) Madeira
350 ml (12 fl oz) chicken stock

To Garnish:
fresh dates
rosemary sprigs

Trim any excess fat and sinew from the meat. Make an incision in the side of the fillet and fill with the dates.

To make the crust, strip the rosemary leaves from their stems and chop them finely; reserve half of the rosemary for the sauce. Place the other half of the rosemary leaves in the food processor with the garlic, breadcrumbs, salt, pepper and half of the melted butter. Process until evenly mixed, adding a little more melted butter if the mixture seems dry. Pat the mixture thickly over the pork and drizzle the remaining melted butter over the top. Roast in a preheated oven at 160°C (325°F) mark 3 for 45 minutes or until the juices run clear, when the thickest part of the meat is pierced with a fine skewer.

To make the sauce, heat 15 g (½ oz) of the butter in a saucepan and sauté the onion until softened, but not coloured.

Add the Madeira, reserved rosemary and chicken stock. Reduce by half. Whisk in the butter cubes, one by one, making sure each piece is thoroughly incorporated before adding the next. Strain the sauce through a sieve and keep warm.

To serve, slice the pork and arrange on warmed serving plates. Garnish with fresh dates and rosemary. Serve with the Madeira sauce, and carrot and leek timbales.

CARROT AND LEEK TIMBALES

575 g (1¼ lb) carrots, cut into large chunks
25 g (1 oz) butter
450 g (1 lb) leeks, finely chopped
1 egg, beaten
salt and freshly ground black pepper

Cook the carrots in a little water until just tender, then drain and chop finely in a food processor.

Melt the butter in a saucepan, add the leeks, cover and sweat gently until softened. Stir in the carrots, egg and seasoning until evenly mixed.

Spoon the mixture into 6 greased dariole moulds then place in a bain-marie (or roasting tin containing enough hot water to come halfway up the sides of the moulds). Cover with a piece of buttered greaseproof paper and cook in a preheated oven at 190°C (375°F) mark 5 for 45 minutes until set. Turn out on to warmed plates to serve.

SABLÉS OF CARAMELISED APPLE RINGS, WITH A BLACKCURRANT COULIS

Biscuits:

50 g (2 oz) plain flour
15 ml (1 tbsp) icing sugar
50 g (2 oz) butter, chilled
½ egg, beaten

Apple Rings:

4 dessert apples
25 g (1 oz) unsalted butter
5 ml (1 tsp) ground cinnamon, or to taste
60 ml (4 tbsp) brown sugar, or to taste

Blackcurrant Coulis:

100 g (3½ oz) granulated sugar
400 g (14 oz) blackcurrants

To Finish:

200 ml (7 fl oz) double cream
icing sugar, for dusting
few drops of vanilla essence

To make the biscuits, put the flour, icing sugar and butter in a food processor and process until the mixture resembles fine breadcrumbs. Add the egg, and process briefly until the mixture holds together and forms a ball. Wrap in cling film and leave to rest in the refrigerator for about 2 hours.

Cut the dough in half and roll out, one piece at a time, to a thickness of 3 mm (⅛ inch). Cut out 8 rounds with an 8 cm (3¼ inch) pastry cutter and place on a lightly buttered large baking tray. (Re-roll the trimmings to cut more rounds as necessary.)

Bake on the middle shelf of a pre-heated oven at 200°C (400°F) mark 6 for 8 minutes, or until the biscuits are golden brown around the edges and firm in the centre. Remove from the oven and transfer to a wire rack to cool. Store in an airtight container until ready to serve.

To make the blackcurrant coulis, put the sugar in a heavy-based saucepan with 30 ml (2 tbsp) water and dissolve over a low heat. Increase the heat and cook until the syrup reaches 154°C (310°F) or until it just begins to colour. Cool slightly, then add the blackcurrants. Return to the heat, bring to the boil and cook for 5 minutes. Remove from the heat and allow to cool until just warm. Purée in a food processor or blender until smooth; pass through a sieve to remove the pips. Allow to cool.

To prepare the apples, peel, core and slice into 5 mm (¼ inch) thick rings. Heat the butter in a sauté pan or frying pan and sauté the apple rings a few at a time, sprinkling with the cinnamon and brown sugar to taste. Cook until the apples are caramelised on the outside but still retain their shape.

To assemble the dessert, whip the cream with a little icing sugar and vanilla essence to taste. Place one biscuit on each serving plate. Arrange 4 apple rings on each of these biscuits, allowing them to overlap the biscuit a little. Put a large spoonful of flavoured cream on top of the apples and cover with another biscuit. Dust with icing sugar and serve with the blackcurrant coulis.

REGIONAL HEATS

THE EAST

RICHARD KUCH • SHIRLEY FAULKNER • HUW WILLIAMS

SHIRLEY FAULKNER'S MENU

STARTER

Individual Salmon and Monkfish Terrines with
a Tomato and Tarragon Dressing
"THE TERRINE WAS EXCELLENT" LOYD

MAIN COURSE

Stuffed Pork Tenderloin in Flaky Pastry,
served with a Cider Sauce

Apple Ratatouille

Braised Chestnuts

DESSERT

Sparkling Melon and Lime Soup

Lacy Tuiles

"THE MELON AND LIME SOUP WAS PRETTY GOOD FUN – MORE OF A
COCKTAIL THAN A PUDDING" LOYD

From Stewkley in Bedfordshire, Shirley Faulkner and her husband Sam run a specialist transport business. Shirley is currently learning to drive the monster vehicles too. For many years Shirley trained as a dancer; she now gives ballet lessons to her daughter Rebecca, and her friends. Shirley and Sam are also leading lights in the Stewkley Players, and are currently in rehearsal for their production of Geoffrey Archer's 'Beyond Reasonable Doubt'.

INDIVIDUAL SALMON AND MONKFISH TERRINES WITH A TOMATO AND TARRAGON DRESSING

8 asparagus spears, trimmed
8 cooked peeled Tiger prawns
300 g (10 oz) skinless salmon fillet
300 g (10 oz) monkfish fillet, trimmed of
* membrane*
30 ml (2 tbsp) white wine
60 ml (4 tbsp) crème fraîche
30 ml (2 tbsp) chopped tarragon
15 ml (1 tbsp) chopped chervil
salt and freshly ground black pepper
1 egg, beaten
dash of Tabasco

Dressing:
225 g (8 oz) tomatoes
1 clove garlic
45 ml (3 tbsp) red wine vinegar
2.5 ml (½ tsp) coarse-grain mustard
salt and freshly ground black pepper
90 ml (6 tbsp) olive oil
15 ml (1 tbsp) chopped tarragon

To Garnish:
lemon twists
cooked whole prawns

Blanch the asparagus spears in boiling water for 2 minutes; drain thoroughly. Arrange the asparagus and prawns attractively in 4 individual 150 ml (¼ pint) loaf tins or similar moulds. Roughly chop the salmon.

Roughly chop the monkfish, then place in a food processor with the wine, 30 ml (2 tbsp) crème fraîche, and the chopped herbs. Season well and add half of the beaten egg. Process until smooth, then divide between the individual tins.

Place the salmon in the processor with the remaining crème fraîche, the rest of the beaten egg, and the Tabasco. Work until smooth, then divide between the tins, spreading it evenly on top of the monkfish filling.

Place the individual tins in a bain-marie or a roasting tin and pour in enough boiling water to come halfway up the sides of the tins. Cover with foil and cook in a preheated oven at 180°C (350°F) mark 4 for 15 minutes or until firm to the touch.

Meanwhile, make the dressing. Skin and roughly chop the tomatoes. Place in a food processor with the garlic, wine vinegar, mustard and seasoning to taste. Process briefly to a pulp (not until smooth). Gradually blend in the oil, in a fine trickle through the feeder tube, as though making mayonnaise. Finally, add the chopped tarragon and process again very briefly. Taste and adjust the seasoning.

To serve, unmould the terrines onto individual serving plates. Garnish with lemon twists and whole prawns. Serve with the tomato and tarragon dressing.

STUFFED PORK TENDERLOIN IN FLAKY PASTRY WITH A CIDER SAUCE

This recipe uses a quick, easy homemade flaky pastry. To ensure the margarine is sufficiently chilled place it in the freezer 1 hour before use.

450 g (1 lb) pork tenderloin (fillet)
30 ml (2 tbsp) oil

Stuffing:
50 g (2 oz) dried peaches
50 g (2 oz) rindless bacon
15 ml (1 tbsp) oil
15 ml (1 tbsp) chopped parsley
25 g (1 oz) pistachio nuts, roughly chopped
50 g (2 oz) fresh breadcrumbs
salt and freshly ground black pepper

Flaky Pastry:
225 g (8 oz) plain flour
pinch of salt
175 g (6 oz) ice-cold margarine (see above)

Cider Sauce:
15 ml (1 tbsp) flour
300 ml (½ pint) dry cider
10 ml (2 tsp) chopped sage

Trim off any excess fat and sinew from the pork. Make a horizontal cut through one side, without cutting right through. Open the pork out and place between two sheets of greaseproof paper or cling film. Using a heavy rolling pin, beat the meat from the centre out to the sides until it is quite thin; set aside.

To make the stuffing, put the peaches in a bowl, pour on boiling water to cover and leave to soak for about 5 minutes. Chop the bacon finely. Heat the oil in a pan and sauté the bacon for a few minutes. Drain and chop the peaches. Add to the pan with the parsley, nuts and breadcrumbs. Mix thoroughly and season with salt and pepper.

Allow to cool, then spread the stuffing along the length of the pork, leaving a margin along the edges. Fold in the ends and bring the sides together to form a roll. Tie securely at 2.5 cm (1 inch) intervals with string.

Heat 30 ml (2 tbsp) oil in a frying pan, add the pork and seal over a high heat, turning to ensure that all sides are sealed. Remove the pork from the pan and leave to cool; reserve the pan juices.

To make the flaky pastry, sift the flour and salt into a mixing bowl. Dip the iced margarine into the flour then, holding it with a piece of foil, grate it using a coarse grater into the flour. You will end up with a huge mound of grated margarine on top of the flour. Using a palette knife, cut the margarine into the flour until evenly mixed and quite crumbly; do not use your hands. Add enough cold water to mix to a dough; pop into a polythene bag and leave to rest in the refrigerator for 30 minutes.

Meanwhile make the cider sauce. Reheat the reserved pork pan juices. Stir in the flour, then gradually stir in the cider. Add the sage and season with salt and pepper. Bring to the boil and boil until thick and syrupy; keep warm.

Roll out the pastry to a rectangle approximately 5 cm (2 inches) larger than the pork. Place the pork in the middle of the pastry. Brush the pastry edges with beaten egg and wrap the pastry around the pork to enclose. Place seam-side down on a baking sheet and decorate with leaves cut from the pastry trimmings. Brush all over with beaten egg and bake in a preheated oven at 220°C (425°F) mark 7 for 15-20 minutes. Cut into slices and serve with the cider sauce, and accompaniments.

APPLE RATATOUILLE

1 aubergine, sliced
2 courgettes, sliced
salt and freshly ground black pepper
15 ml (1 tbsp) oil
1 large onion, sliced
1 clove garlic, crushed
1 red pepper, seeded and sliced
400 g (14 oz) can chopped tomatoes
15 ml (1 tbsp) chopped basil
450 g (1 lb) cooking apples

Slice the aubergine and courgettes and place in a colander. Sprinkle liberally with salt and leave for 30 minutes to draw out any bitter juices and excess moisture. Rinse well and pat dry with kitchen paper.

Heat the oil in a large saucepan, add the onion and garlic and fry gently until softened. Add the red pepper, courgettes and aubergine and cook, stirring, for a few minutes. Add the tomatoes, chopped basil and seasoning and simmer gently for 10 minutes. Peel, core and slice the apples. Add to the pan and simmer gently for about 5 minutes until the apples are just soft.

Note: Do not let the vegetables soften too much during cooking – they should retain their shape.

BRAISED CHESTNUTS

12 fresh chestnuts
1 celery stick, chopped
1 bouquet garni
5 ml (1 tsp) sugar
salt and freshly ground black pepper

Nick the outer skin of each chestnut with a sharp knife and place in a saucepan of boiling water for a few minutes. Remove the chestnuts with a slotted spoon and peel off both the outer and inner skins.

Place the peeled chestnuts in a saucepan with 600 ml (1 pint) water, the celery, bouquet garni, sugar and salt and pepper. Cover and simmer for 40-45 minutes until the chestnuts are tender. Drain thoroughly and serve.

SPARKLING MELON AND LIME SOUP

1 ripe Galia or Charentais melon
finely pared rind and juice of 2 dark green
  limes
25 g (1 oz) sugar
90 ml (6 tbsp) Champagne or sparkling wine

To Decorate:
strawberries
mint sprigs

Halve the melon and scoop out 350 g (12 oz) flesh, reserving the juice. Squeeze out extra juice from the melon to yield 150 ml (¼ pint); if necessary make up to this quantity with water. Pour the melon juice into a saucepan. Add the pared lime rind and sugar. Bring to the boil and boil for 2-3 minutes.

Allow to cool, then strain into a blender or food processor. Add the melon flesh and lime juice and work to a purée. Divide between individual serving bowls and chill before serving.

Just before serving, carefully add the Champagne or sparkling wine and decorate with strawberries and mint sprigs. Serve with lacy tuiles.

LACY TUILES

75 g (3 oz) butter, softened
75 g (3 oz) caster sugar
50 g (2 oz) plain flour
pinch of salt

In a bowl, beat the butter and sugar together until light and fluffy. Stir in the flour and salt.

Place teaspoonfuls of the mixture on a greased baking tray, spacing them well apart. Flatten with the back of a spoon. Bake in a preheated oven at 200°C (400°F) mark 6 for 5-6 minutes until golden brown.

Remove from the oven and while still hot, curl over a small rolling pin. Leave until firm, then carefully remove and place on a wire rack to cool completely.

REGIONAL HEATS
THE EAST
RICHARD KUCH • SHIRLEY FAULKNER • HUW WILLIAMS

HUW WILLIAMS' MENU

STARTER
*Lemon Sole and Langoustines with a Carrot and
Coriander Sauce*

MAIN COURSE
*Mignons of Venison served with a Sauce of Redcurrant
and Caramelised Apple
Sorrel Crêpes filled with a Parsnip Purée
Seasonal Vegetables*

DESSERT
White Cheese Mousse, with Exotic Fruits and Fruit Coulis
"I LIKE THE FACT THAT THE SAUCE IS NOT SWEET" LOYD

Huw Williams from Leighton Buzzard in Bedfordshire is an executive with Reuters. As light relief from his high pressure job, Huw enjoys go-karting. Of an evening he can sometimes be found in his favourite wine bar, enjoying the vintages with his friends.

LEMON SOLE AND LANGOUSTINES WITH A CARROT AND CORIANDER SAUCE

4 lemon sole fillets, skinned
1 bunch of coriander, stalks removed
50 g (2 oz) carrot
150 ml (¼ pint) court bouillon (see right)
20 cooked, shelled langoustines
50 g (2 oz) chilled butter, in pieces
juice of ½ lemon, or to taste
salt and freshly ground white pepper

Cut the sole fillets into strips, 1 x 2.5 cm (½ x 1 inch). Set aside 16-20 coriander leaves for the garnish; finely chop the remainder. Cut the carrot into julienne strips.

Bring the court bouillon to the boil in a saucepan, add the sole and cook for 1-2 minutes. Add the chopped coriander and allow to infuse for a few seconds. Add the langoustines and cook for a further 1-2 minutes. Remove the fish from the liquid and keep warm.

Strain the cooking liquid and discard half of it. Return the other half to the cleaned pan and gradually whisk in the butter a piece at a time, making sure each piece is thoroughly incorporated before adding the next. Add the carrot julienne, lemon juice and seasoning. Cook for about 1 minute to soften the carrot.

To serve, arrange the sole and langoustines on warmed serving plates on a pool of the sauce. Arrange the reserved coriander leaves on the sauce.

COURT BOUILLON

This recipe yields approximately 600 ml (1 pint) court bouillon.

1 small onion
½ leek
1 celery stick
2 carrots
3 cloves garlic, halved
2 lemon slices
few white peppercorns
1 star anise
1 bay leaf
1 sprig each of parsley, coriander and
*   tarragon*
90 ml (3 fl oz) white wine

Coarsely chop the vegetables and place in a saucepan with the garlic, lemon slices, peppercorns and star anise. Add 600 ml (1 pint) cold water and bring to the boil. Lower the heat and simmer, covered, for 8 minutes.

Add the herbs, simmer for 2 minutes, then remove from the heat and add the wine. Leave to infuse for several hours, or overnight if possible. Strain the court bouillon before use.

MIGNONS OF VENISON WITH A SAUCE OF REDCURRANT AND CARAMELISED APPLE

675 g (1½ lb) fillet or 'eye of silverside' of venison
300 ml (½ pint) demi-glace (see right)
30-45 ml (2-3 tbsp) crème de cassis
125 g (4 oz) redcurrants
2 Granny Smith apples
oil and butter, for frying
salt and freshly ground black pepper
50 g (2 oz) chilled butter, in pieces

Trim the venison if necessary. To make the sauce, pour the demi-glace into a saucepan and add the crème de cassis and half of the redcurrants. Bring to the boil and simmer until well reduced. Keep warm.

Peel the apples and, using a melon baller, scoop 8 balls from the apple flesh. Fry the apple balls in a little butter until golden.

Season the venison with salt and pepper. Heat a little oil and butter in a frying pan, add the venison and fry for 7 minutes, turning to brown evenly. Remove from the pan and cut the venison into 2.5 cm (1 inch) mignons. Return these to the pan and fry for 2-3 minutes on each side, or until cooked to your liking.

Meanwhile, bring the sauce to a simmer. Remove the redcurrants with a slotted spoon and discard. Add the remaining redcurrants to the sauce and poach briefly for a few seconds; remove with a slotted spoon and set aside for the garnish. Gradually whisk the butter into the sauce, a piece at a time, making sure each piece is thoroughly incorporated before adding the next. Check the seasoning.

Arrange the venison mignons on warmed serving plates. Spoon plenty of sauce over and around the meat. Place a bunch of redcurrants to one side of the venison, and the caramelised apples to the other side. Serve immediately, with the accompaniments.

DEMI-GLACE

This should be made the day before it is needed. This recipe yields about 300 ml (½ pint) demi-glace.

600 ml (1 pint) veal stock
175 g (6 oz) shallots, chopped
225 g (8 oz) carrots, chopped
175 g (6 oz) onions, chopped
175 g (6 oz) celery, chopped
15 g (½ oz) dried herbs de Provence
150 ml (¼ pint) port
150 ml (¼ pint) red wine
90 ml (3 fl oz) Madeira
freshly ground black pepper

Pour the veal stock into a saucepan and reduce by one third, then skim. Add all the other ingredients, bring to the boil and simmer until reduced by one third. Strain through a sieve and refrigerate until required.

SORREL CRÊPES FILLED WITH A PARSNIP PURÉE

Crêpe Batter:
50 g (2 oz) plain flour
pinch of salt
2.5 ml (½ tsp) freshly grated nutmeg
1 egg, beaten
150 ml (¼ pint) milk
15 g (½ oz) butter, melted
butter, for frying

Parsnip Purée:
450 g (1 lb) parsnips
50 g (2 oz) butter
salt and freshly ground white pepper
50 g (2 oz) sorrel
150 ml (¼ pint) double cream

To make the crêpe batter, mix the flour, salt, nutmeg and egg in a bowl and gradually whisk in the milk. Allow to stand while preparing the filling.

To make the parsnip purée, finely dice the parsnips. Melt the butter in a heavy-based saucepan, add the parsnips and season with salt. Cover and cook gently, stirring occasionally, until tender. Purée in a blender or food processor until smooth.

Remove the stalks from the sorrel, roll up the leaves and chop finely. Add 15 ml (1 tbsp) chopped sorrel to the crêpe batter with the melted butter; mix thoroughly.

Pour the cream into a saucepan and bring to the boil. Add the rest of the chopped sorrel, lower the heat and simmer for 5 minutes. Stir into the puréed parsnips, ensuring the mixture is well amalgamated. Season with salt and pepper to taste.

Heat a little butter in a crêpe pan, add a spoonful of batter, tilt to coat the base of the pan evenly; each crêpe should be 12-15 cm (5-6 inches) in diameter. Cook until golden underneath, then turn and cook the other side. Repeat with the rest of the batter, stacking the crêpes interleaved with greaseproof paper as they are cooked.

Trim the crêpes to neaten if necessary. Place a spoonful of parsnip and sorrel purée in the middle of each crêpe and fold the edges over the filling to make parcels. Place the parcels, seam-side down, on a baking tray. Reheat in a moderate oven at 180°C (350°F) mark 4 for 12-15 minutes before serving.

White Cheese Mousse with Exotic Fruits and Fruit Coulis

Coulis:
2 ripe mangos
2 papayas
a little kirsch (optional)
a little sparkling mineral water

White Cheese Mousse:
4 gelatine leaves
45 ml (3 tbsp) milk
400 g (14 oz) fromage frais
100 g (3½ oz) caster sugar
200 ml (7 fl oz) double cream, lightly
  whipped

To Decorate:
mint leaves

Peel the mangos with a sharp knife and, using a melon baller, scoop 16-20 balls of fruit. Soak these in a little kirsch, if desired. To make the mango coulis, cut the remaining mango flesh from the stones and purée in a blender until smooth. Add a little mineral water and flavour with a little kirsch if liked. Pass through a nylon sieve into a bowl, cover and chill in the refrigerator.

Peel the papayas, halve and scoop out the seeds. Scoop out 16-20 balls, as for the melon, soaking in kirsch if wished. To make the papaya coulis, purée the remaining papaya flesh until smooth, adding a little mineral water and kirsch if wished. Cover and chill in the refrigerator.

To make the mousse, soak the gelatine leaves in a little cold water until soft, then squeeze out excess water. Carefully dissolve the gelatine in the milk over a very low heat. In a bowl, whisk the fromage frais and sugar together until very smooth. Whisk in the dissolved gelatine, then fold in the whipped cream. Leave in the refrigerator for 3-4 hours until set.

To assemble the dessert, spoon the mango coulis onto one side of each plate; spoon the papaya coulis onto the opposite side. Rapidly twist each plate so that the coulis meet and form an attractive pattern. Using two spoons, shape the white cheese mousse into oval quenelles and place on the coulis. Arrange the mango and papaya balls on the plate and decorate with mint leaves. Serve immediately.

REGIONAL HEATS

THE NORTH

RACHEL SOUTHALL • JULIETTE FORDEN • TIMOTHY STOKES

WINNER

RACHEL SOUTHALL'S MENU

STARTER

*Medley of Mushrooms in Filo Pastry Parcels, served
with a Butter Sauce*

MAIN COURSE

*Halibut Escalopes with Courgettes
Seasonal Vegetables*

"A REALLY TERRIFIC COMBINATION ... AND THE FISH DIDN'T
LOSE ITS MEATINESS" ROSE GREY

DESSERT

Pears in Sauternes, with a Ginger and Chocolate Sauce

"IF WE WEREN'T ON TV, I WOULD HAVE WOLFED
THIS DOWN!" ALAN COREN

R achel Southall from Sheffield is a staff nurse at
the Jessop Hospital where she cares for premature
babies in the neonatal ward. She is an enthusiastic swimmer
and a regular visitor to the Olympic pool at the Ponds Forge
centre. A devout Christian, Rachel spends much of her spare
time at Christ Church, Fulwood, where she is a leading
member of the music group.

MEDLEY OF MUSHROOMS IN FILO PARCELS, WITH A BUTTER SAUCE

Use a mixture of different mushrooms for these filo parcels, such as oyster, chestnut and cup mushrooms.

175 g (6 oz) butter
50 g (2 oz) onion, chopped
1 clove garlic, crushed
225 g (8 oz) mushrooms, finely chopped
15 ml (1 tbsp) snipped chives
15 ml (1 tbsp) red wine
salt and freshly ground black pepper
225 g (8 oz) packet filo pastry
120 ml (4 fl oz) dry white wine
120 ml (4 fl oz) double cream

Melt 50 g (2 oz) of the butter in a pan. Add the onion, garlic, mushrooms, chives and red wine. Season with salt and pepper. Cook for 2 minutes, then strain off excess liquid into another pan. Set aside the mushrooms and reserved liquid.

Cut the filo pastry into 10 cm (4 inch) squares; you will need 36 squares. Melt 50 g (2 oz) butter. Brush the filo squares lightly with melted butter and layer them in threes, on top of each other at an angle to make 12 piles.

Place a teaspoonful of the mushroom mixture in the middle of each filo pile. Bring the edges of the pastry up over the filling to form little parcels and pinch together to secure. Place on greased baking sheets and brush lightly with melted butter. Bake in a preheated oven at 200°C (400°F) mark 6 for about 3-4 minutes, or until the pastry is crisp and golden.

Meanwhile, place the saucepan containing the mushroom cooking liquor over a medium heat, add the white wine and bring to the boil. Lower the heat slightly and add the cream, then simmer to reduce by one third. Remove from the heat and slowly whisk in the remaining 50 g (2 oz) butter, a small piece at a time, making sure each piece is thoroughly incorporated before adding the next.

Pour the sauce on to warmed serving plates, arrange the parcels on top and serve immediately.

Note: If preferred you could tie chives or fine strips of leek around the filo parcels to make them look more attractive.

HALIBUT ESCALOPES WITH COURGETTES

Rachel based this dish on an original recipe from Anton Mosimann's *"Fish Cuisine"*, first published in 1988.

If possible, get your fishmonger to bone and skin the halibut for you, but remember to ask for the bones and skin for your fish stock.

575 g (1¼ lb) halibut fillet, skinned
salt and freshly ground black pepper
300 g (10 oz) courgettes
250 ml (8 fl oz) fish stock
100 ml (3½ fl oz) dry white wine
1 egg yolk
225 ml (7½ fl oz) double cream
30 g (1 oz) butter
30 ml (1 tbsp) fresh white breadcrumbs
30 ml (1 tbsp) freshly grated Parmesan
*   cheese*

Cut the fish diagonally into 6 mm (¼ inch) thick slices and season with salt and pepper; set aside. Cut the courgettes lengthwise into 3 mm (⅛ inch) slices, using a cheese slicer, then blanch in boiling water for a few seconds; drain thoroughly.

Combine the fish stock and white wine in a saucepan and boil rapidly to reduce by half. Meanwhile mix the egg yolk with 30 ml (2 tbsp) of the cream; strain through a fine sieve and set aside. Add the remaining cream to the stock mixture and reduce again by half. Remove from the heat and carefully stir in the cream and egg mixture; don't let the sauce cook again or it will separate. Season with salt and pepper to taste.

Brush 4 large flat flameproof plates with butter and sprinkle them with salt and pepper. Fold the courgette slices in half and arrange on the plates. Lay the thin slices of fish on top and coat with the sauce. Sprinkle with the breadcrumbs and Parmesan. Season with a little pepper and place the plates under a hot grill for about 1 minute or until the topping is golden brown and the fish is cooked through. Serve immediately.

PEARS IN SAUTERNES, WITH A GINGER AND CHOCOLATE SAUCE

4 ripe firm pears
250 ml (8 fl oz) Sauternes wine
25 g (1 oz) sugar
juice of ½ lemon

Sauce:
100 g (3½ oz) plain dark chocolate
30 g (1 oz) preserved stem ginger in syrup,
*   drained*

Peel the pears, leaving the stalks on. Carefully remove the cores from the base of the pears, using an apple corer or teaspoon.

Pour the Sauternes into a saucepan. Add 250 ml (8 fl oz) water, the sugar and lemon juice. Heat gently until the sugar has dissolved. Bring to the boil, then stand the pears in the liquid. Cover and simmer for 15-30 minutes depending on the ripeness of the pears, until they are translucent. Lift the pears out of the liquid and leave to cool; reserve the cooking liquid.

Meanwhile melt the chocolate in a heatproof bowl over a pan of simmering water. Finely chop the ginger and add to the melted chocolate. Stir in enough of the reserved liquid to give a smooth pouring consistency. Pour some of the sauce on to each serving plate and place a pear in the middle. Serve immediately.

Note: To test the pears insert a fine skewer into the base of each one.

Pecan and Chestnut Casserole in Red Wine
JANET DIMMER'S MAIN COURSE (REGIONAL HEAT)

Lavender Baked Figs on Brioche Toasts
BRIAN TOMPKINS' DESSERT (SEMI-FINAL)

REGIONAL HEATS
THE NORTH

RACHEL SOUTHALL • JULIETTE FORDEN • TIMOTHY STOKES

JULIETTE FORDEN'S MENU

STARTER

Cauliflower and White Stilton Soup

Toast Rounds

"THIS SOUP'S GOT LEGS ... THE FLAVOURS REALLY LINGER" ALAN COREN

MAIN COURSE

Celebration Nut Roast en Croûte

Fantail Lemon Garlic Potatoes

Julienne of Carrot with Dill

Vegetarian Gravy

DESSERT

Apricot Streusels, served with Amaretto and Apricot Sauce,
and Greek Yogurt Cream

Juliette Forden from Durham is a practising masseuse, specialising in curing the injuries and ailments which befall racing cyclists. Juliette is a keen cyclist too and her professional advice is often sought on race days. Juliette is also currently studying for her Physics A level at York college.

CAULIFLOWER AND WHITE STILTON SOUP

50 g (2 oz) butter
225 g (8 oz) cauliflower florets
125 g (4 oz) onion, finely chopped
125 g (4 oz) leeks, finely chopped
125 g (4 oz) celery, finely chopped
50 g (2 oz) potatoes, finely chopped
50 g (2 oz) plain flour
*1 bouquet garni, (bay leaf, thyme and
   peppercorns)*
600 ml (1 pint) vegetable stock
450 ml (¾ pint) milk
175 g (6 oz) white Stilton cheese
150 ml (¼ pint) double cream
freshly ground black pepper
30 ml (2 tbsp) yogurt
15 ml (1 tbsp) chopped parsley

Melt the butter in a large heavy-based pan. Add the cauliflower, onion, leeks, celery and potatoes, cover and sweat in the butter until transparent but not coloured. Stir in the flour and cook gently for 5 minutes.

Add the bouquet garni, stock and milk. Cover and simmer for about 30 minutes. Remove the bay leaf and bouquet garni.

Crumble the cheese and add to the soup, then stir in the cream. Season with pepper to taste; salt is unnecessary because the Stilton provides sufficient.

Divide between warmed soup plates and swirl in the yogurt. Sprinkle with chopped parsley and serve immediately, with toast rounds.

Note: If preferred, purée the soup before adding the cheese and cream.

CELEBRATION NUT ROAST EN CROÛTE

Shortcrust Pastry:

350 g (12 oz) plain flour
210 g (7½ oz) butter, in pieces
90 ml (6 tbsp) water (approximately)
beaten egg, to glaze

Nut Roast:

50 g (2 oz) butter
2 large onions, finely chopped
450 g (1 lb) Brazil nuts, finely grated
225 g (8 oz) soft fine white breadcrumbs
5 ml (1 tsp) chopped thyme
45 ml (3 tbsp) lemon juice
large pinch of freshly grated nutmeg
large pinch of ground cloves
large pinch of ground cinnamon
salt and freshly ground black pepper
1 egg, beaten, and a little water to mix

Stuffing:

225 g (8 oz) soft fine white breadcrumbs
25 g (1 oz) chopped parsley
15 ml (1 tbsp) lemon juice
finely grated rind of 1 lemon
10 ml (2 tsp) chopped thyme
10 ml (2 tsp) chopped marjoram
15 ml (1 tbsp) grated onion
75 g (3 oz) butter, melted

To Serve:

Vegetarian Gravy (see overleaf)

To make the pastry, put the flour in a food processor, add the butter and process until the mixture resembles fine breadcrumbs. Add sufficient water through the feeder tube to bind, mixing briefly until the dough comes together. Wrap in cling film and leave to rest in the refrigerator for 30 minutes.

To prepare the nut roast, melt the butter in a pan, add the onions and fry until softened but not brown. Remove from the heat. Add all the rest of the nut roast ingredients, seasoning well and making sure that the mixture is sufficiently moist.

For the stuffing, mix all the ingredients together to make a soft mixture which holds together; season carefully with salt and pepper.

Roll out the shortcrust pastry on a lightly floured surface to a rectangle, 30 x 35 cm (12 x 14 inches). Spoon one third of the nut roast along the middle of the pastry. Form the stuffing into a sausage and place along the middle of the nut roast. Pile the remaining nut roast mixture over the stuffing. Make parallel slits in the pastry at 4 cm (1½ inch) intervals along both sides of the nut roast. Brush with beaten egg and plait these strips over the top of the nut roast.

Place the nut roast on a baking sheet lined with greaseproof paper. Cover and leave to rest for 15 minutes. Brush with beaten egg to glaze and cook in a preheated oven at 200°C (400°F) mark 6 for about 30 minutes until crisp and golden brown. Serve with vegetarian gravy and the accompaniments.

VEGETARIAN GRAVY

30 ml (2 tbsp) olive oil
1 onion, chopped
1 stick celery, finely chopped
30 ml (2 tbsp) plain flour
1 clove garlic, crushed
600 ml (1 pint) dark vegetarian stock
2.5 ml (½ tsp) mustard powder
2 bay leaves
5 ml (1 tsp) chopped fresh thyme or ½ tsp
  dried thyme
30 ml (1 tbsp) soy sauce
7.5 ml (1½ tsp) miso
salt and freshly ground black pepper

Heat the oil in a pan, add the onion and celery and fry for 5 minutes. Add the flour and cook for 5-10 minutes, until the flour, onion and celery are nut brown and soft. Add the garlic and cook for 1-2 minutes.

Gradually stir in the vegetarian stock, mustard, bay leaves and thyme. Bring to the boil and simmer for 15 minutes. Strain the gravy into a clean pan. Add the soy sauce, miso, salt and pepper to taste. Stir well and serve.

FANTAIL LEMON GARLIC POTATOES

12 evenly-sized medium potatoes
45 ml (3 tbsp) olive oil
2 cloves garlic, crushed
30 ml (2 tbsp) lemon juice

Peel and turn the potatoes, by trimming to a uniform shape, with seven sides.

Mix the oil and crushed garlic together in a large bowl and leave for a little while for the garlic to infuse the oil.

Push a skewer through the base of the potatoes, then slice the potatoes lengthwise at narrow intervals, cutting almost but not quite through to the base. (The skewer helps to prevent cutting right through.) Remove the skewer and place the potatoes in a bowl of cold water.

Strain the oil through a sieve to remove the garlic, then add the lemon juice. Drain the potatoes and pat dry with kitchen paper, then add to the oil mixture, turning them to ensure the potatoes are evenly coated with flavoured oil.

Place the potatoes in a baking sheet lined with non-stick baking parchment. Cook in a preheated oven at 200°C (400°F) mark 6 for 35-40 minutes or until golden brown, basting occasionally.

APRICOT STREUSELS

Streusel Pastry:
150 g (5 oz) plain flour
pinch of salt
50 g (2 oz) caster sugar
75 g (3 oz) butter
2 egg yolks

Filling:
150 g (5 oz) plain flour
25 g (1 oz) ground almonds
75 g (3 oz) butter
50 g (2 oz) caster sugar
45 ml (3 tbsp) apricot jam
400 g (14 oz) can apricots, drained

Yogurt Cream:
175 ml (6 fl oz) Greek-style yogurt
175 ml (6 fl oz) double cream

Amaretto and Apricot Sauce:
60 ml (4 tbsp) apricot jam
30 ml (2 tbsp) Amaretto di Saronno liqueur

To make the streusel pastry, sift the flour and salt onto a work surface and make a well in the centre. Place the sugar, butter and egg yolks in the well. Using the fingertips of one hand, gradually work the ingredients together to form a firm dough. Knead lightly and wrap in cling film. Leave to rest in a cool place for 20 minutes.

For the filling, mix the flour and ground almonds together in a bowl. Rub in the butter until the mixture resembles fine breadcrumbs. Stir in the sugar.

Roll out the streusel pastry and cut out 4 circles to fit the bases of four 7.5 cm (3 inch) flan rings. Butter and flour the rings and place on a lightly greased baking sheet. Lay the pastry circles in the bottom of the flan rings. Prick well and spread with the apricot jam.

Place half of the apricots on the jam and cover with a layer of the crumbed mixture. Arrange the remaining apricots on top and sprinkle with the rest of the crumbed mixture. Press down lightly with the fingertips.

Bake in a preheated oven at 200°C (400°F) mark 6 for 15 minutes, then lower the oven temperature to 160°C (325°F) mark 3 and bake for a further 20-25 minutes.

Meanwhile prepare the yogurt cream. Spoon the yogurt into a sieve lined with a piece of kitchen paper. Place the sieve over a bowl and leave to drain through for at least 30 minutes. In a bowl whip the cream until just thick; do not over-whip. Fold in the drained yogurt. Chill before serving.

For the amaretto and apricot sauce, place the jam, amaretto liqueur and 30 ml (2 tbsp) water in a saucepan and stir well. Bring to the boil slowly over a low heat. Strain through a sieve.

Remove the rings from the streusels and serve hot or cold, with the amaretto and apricot sauce and the yogurt cream.

REGIONAL HEATS
THE NORTH
RACHEL SOUTHALL • JULIETTE FORDEN • TIMOTHY STOKES

TIMOTHY STOKES' MENU

STARTER
Scallops with a Ginger and Soy Butter Sauce
"THE SCALLOPS ARE WONDERFULLY MUSCULAR AND STAND UP
WELL TO THE ORIENTAL SAUCE" ALAN COREN

MAIN COURSE
Lamb with a Garlic and Redcurrant Sauce
Pan-fried Rosemary Potatoes
Creamed Leeks
Caramelised Shallots

DESSERT
Passion Fruit Soufflé
"VERY GOOD! ABSOLUTELY EXQUISITE TASTE. THIS IS MY
FAVOURITE KIND OF PUDDING." ROSE GREY

Timothy Stokes from Harrogate in North Yorkshire is a quantity surveyor. Outside work hours Tim is a regular at the local gym. His hobbies include shooting and fly fishing in the river Wharfe.

SCALLOPS WITH A GINGER AND SOY BUTTER SAUCE

If possible buy large fresh scallops, with shells approximately 12 cm (5 inches) across.

4 large scallops
100 ml (3½ fl oz) Noilly Prat
julienne of fresh root ginger
soy sauce, to taste (see note)
15 g (½ oz) unsalted butter, chilled
salt and freshly ground black pepper
juice of ½ lemon, to taste
6 coriander leaves, finely shredded
chervil sprigs, to garnish

Remove the scallops from their shells and clean thoroughly, discarding the grey beard-like fringe, black thread and intestinal sac. Cut each scallop horizontally into three slices.

Put the Noilly Prat in a saucepan, add the scallops and poach gently for no longer than 2 minutes each side; do not boil. Remove the scallops with a slotted spoon and transfer to a warm plate; cover and keep warm.

Add the ginger and soy sauce to the Noilly Prat. Whisk in the butter, a piece at a time. Add seasoning and lemon juice to taste. At the last minute, add the shredded coriander.

To serve, arrange the scallops on warmed serving plates and spoon the sauce over them. Garnish with chervil.

Note: To make this soy sauce you should use 1 part quality bottled soy sauce to 2 parts old sherry vinegar. Simmer until reduced by half. This soy sauce can then be bottled.

LAMB WITH A GARLIC AND REDCURRANT SAUCE

Flavour the sauce with mint and redcurrant jelly to taste – the more jelly you add, the sweeter the taste.

2 best ends of lamb, each with 7 cutlets
salt and freshly ground black pepper
15 g (½ oz) butter
15 ml (1 tbsp) olive oil

Redcurrant and Garlic Sauce:
300 ml (½ pint) lamb or chicken stock
6 cloves garlic
100 ml (3½ fl oz) Madeira
200 ml (7 fl oz) dry white wine
15-30 ml (1-2 tbsp) chopped mint
30-45 ml (2-3 tbsp) good redcurrant jelly
knob of butter

Trim the lamb if necessary and season with salt and pepper. Preheat a skillet or large heavy-based frying pan and add the butter and oil. Quickly sear the lamb on all sides over a high heat, then place, fat side uppermost, in a roasting tin.

Cook in a preheated oven at 200°C (400°F) mark 6 for about 15 minutes until tender but still pink inside. To test, insert a skewer into the middle of the meat – it should feel warm when removed.

While the lamb is cooking, make the sauce. Bring the stock to the boil in a saucepan. Add the whole garlic cloves, Madeira and white wine. Boil steadily to reduce by about half. Strain, discarding the garlic, then return the sauce to the pan and bring back to the boil. Add chopped mint and redcurrant jelly to taste. Adjust the seasoning. Add a knob of butter just before serving.

Allow the meat to rest in a warm place for a few minutes before carving. Serve with the redcurrant and garlic sauce, and accompaniments.

PAN-FRIED ROSEMARY POTATOES

4 large potatoes
knob of unsalted butter
15 ml (1 tbsp) olive oil
4 rosemary sprigs

Peel the potatoes, trim the edges square, then cut into small cubes and place in cold water. Just before cooking, drain and pat dry with kitchen paper.

Heat the butter and oil in a large heavy-based pan. Add the potato cubes with the rosemary and cook, tossing frequently, until the potatoes are crisp and brown on the outside and cooked through. Drain on absorbent kitchen paper. Serve immediately.

PASSION FRUIT SOUFFLÉ

2 egg yolks
150 g (5 oz) caster sugar
4 egg whites
finely grated rind of ½ lemon

Sauce:

12 passion fruit
65 g (2½ oz) caster sugar
juice of ½ lemon
juice of 1 orange

To Finish:

icing sugar, for dusting

First make the sauce. Cut the passion fruit in half and scoop out the pulp and seeds. Press through a nylon sieve to extract the seeds. Reserve 30 ml (2 tbsp) of the strained juice. Put the rest of the juice and the seeds in a pan with the sugar, the lemon and orange juices and 5 ml (1 tsp) water. Bring to the boil and simmer for 2 minutes. Strain through a sieve and set aside.

Place a roasting tin half-filled with hot water in a preheated oven at 220°C (425°F) mark 7 to heat. Grease a 12 cm (5 inch) soufflé dish with melted butter and sprinkle lightly with caster sugar.

In a bowl, beat the egg yolks with half of the sugar until pale and fluffy. In another bowl, whisk the egg whites with half of the remaining sugar until they start to thicken. Add the rest of the sugar and whisk to a soft peak consistency.

Mix 30 ml (2 tbsp) of the passion fruit syrup (not the reserved juice) with the grated lemon rind. Stir into the egg yolk mixture, then gently fold in one third of the whisked egg whites. Lightly fold in the remaining egg whites.

Pour the mixture into the prepared soufflé dish and place in the roasting tin. Bake for 10-15 minutes until risen and brown.

To serve, add the reserved passion fruit juice to the passion fruit syrup. Heat gently to warm through. When the soufflé is ready, dust with icing sugar and serve immediately, with the warm passion fruit sauce.

Regional Heats

The South East

HELEN WELLER • CAROL BARTLETT • MARC HADLEY

— Winner —

HELEN WELLER'S MENU

STARTER

Skate Wings with a Soy Vinaigrette and Salad

"THIS IS THE SORT OF FIRST COURSE EVERYONE LIKES – LIGHT
AND CLEAN" LOYD

MAIN COURSE

Rabbit with Wild Mushroom Sauce

Timbales of Spinach

Lemon Wild Rice Risotto

DESSERT

Apricot and Amaretto Mousse Brulée

"THIS MENU HAS JUST THE RIGHT BALANCE" PRUE LEITH

Helen Weller lives in Andover, Hampshire. Helen is a hairdresser in a fashionable Reading salon which she runs with her husband, Gary. Helen is a regular at the Sindlesham Sports Club where she throws herself enthusiastically into the punishing aerobic sessions. Helen is equally serious about her wine; she and Gary often attend wine tastings.

SKATE WING WITH A SOY VINAIGRETTE AND SALAD

575 g (1¼ lb) skate wing
65 g (2½ oz) butter, melted
30 ml (2 tbsp) soy sauce
5-10 ml (1-2 tsp) chopped tarragon
½ leek (white part only)
½ stick celery
1 carrot
1 courgette
salt and freshly ground black pepper
2 shallots, finely chopped
300 ml (½ pint) fish stock
15 ml (1 tbsp) oil
15 ml (1 tbsp) tarragon vinegar
1 bunch of chives, snipped

Salad:
100 g (3½ oz) young spinach leaves
100 g (3½ oz) rocket
175 g (6 oz) frisée
2 tomatoes, skinned, seeded and diced

Place the skate on a large piece of foil. Flavour 50 g (2 oz) of the butter with a little of the soy sauce and chopped tarragon and brush over the fish. Cut the leek, celery, carrot and courgette into julienne strips and sprinkle over the fish. Season with salt and pepper. Wrap tightly to form a parcel, sealing the edges well. Place in the top of a steamer and steam for 5 minutes or until the fish is cooked. Meanwhile sweat the shallots in the remaining butter until softened.

Skin and fillet the skate, reserving the cooking juices and vegetable julienne, keep warm. Pour the fish stock and cooking juices into a pan, bring to the boil and reduce by half, then strain.

Whisk together the oil, vinegar and remaining tarragon, then whisk 15 ml (1 tbsp) of this dressing into the sauce to enrich it. Add half of the shallots, chives and remaining soy sauce to the sauce. And the other half of these ingredients to the dressing.

Arrange the salad leaves around the edge of the serving plates and brush with the dressing. Place the skate fillets in the centre, spoon on the sauce and sprinkle with the vegetable julienne and diced tomatoes. Serve immediately.

RABBIT WITH WILD MUSHROOM SAUCE

5 large shallots
3 cloves garlic
125 g (4 oz) butter
1 thyme sprig
½ bay leaf
12 g (½ oz) dried mushrooms, crushed
400 g (14 oz) white button mushrooms
200 ml (7 fl oz) white wine
100 ml (3½ fl oz) Madeira
300 ml (½ pint) chicken stock
2 saddles of rabbit
150 ml (¼ pint) whipping cream

Finely slice the shallots and garlic. Melt 40 g (1½ oz) of the butter in a pan. Add the shallots and garlic with the thyme, bay leaf and dried mushrooms. Cook until the shallots are opaque.

Meanwhile coarsely slice the button mushrooms. Add to the pan and cook, stirring, until all excess liquid has evaporated.

Add the white wine and reduce by half. Add the Madeira. Pour in the chicken stock, bring to the boil and simmer for 20 minutes. Strain the sauce, then return to the pan and reduce by half.

Meanwhile, heat another 50 g (2 oz) butter in a frying pan and brown the saddles of rabbit quickly on all sides. Remove from the pan, wrap in foil and cook in a preheated oven at 190°C (375°F) mark 5 for 10-15 minutes. Leave to rest in the foil for 5 minutes. To finish the sauce, stir in the cream, then whisk in the remaining 15 g (½ oz) chilled butter, a piece at a time.

Slice the rabbit and arrange on warmed serving plates. Spoon the sauce over the rabbit and serve immediately, with the accompaniments.

TIMBALES OF SPINACH

200 g (7 oz) spinach leaves
15 ml (1 tbsp) melted butter

Blanch the spinach leaves in boiling water for 2 minutes. Drain thoroughly, then toss in the melted butter. Press the spinach into 4 warmed buttered dariole moulds. Turn out the timbales and serve immediately.

LEMON WILD RICE RISOTTO

100 g (3½ oz) wild rice
salt and freshly ground black pepper
30 g (1 oz) brown rice
15 g (½ oz) butter
2 shallots, chopped
1 bacon rasher, derinded and chopped
1 clove garlic, crushed
finely grated rind of 1 lemon
100 g (3½ oz) chicken stock

Cook the wild rice in plenty of boiling salted water for 30 minutes. Add the brown rice to the pan and cook for a further 20 minutes or until tender. Drain and cool.

Heat the butter in a pan, add the shallots, bacon and garlic and cook until the shallots are softened. Add the lemon rind, chicken stock and rice. Mix well, then divide the mixture between 4 buttered moulds. Bake in a preheated oven at 190°C (375°F) mark 5 for 5 minutes. Turn out onto warmed plates to serve.

APRICOT AND AMARETTO MOUSSE BRULÉE

200 g (7 oz) caster sugar
30 g (1 oz) flaked almonds
400 ml (14 fl oz) double cream
½ vanilla pod
4 egg yolks
30 ml (2 tbsp) Amaretto di Saronno liqueur
8 preserved apricots, drained (see note)

Dissolve 150 g (5 oz) of the sugar in 25 ml (1½ tbsp) water in a heavy-based pan over low heat. Increase the heat and cook until the syrup turns golden brown. Add the flaked almonds and cook for 30 seconds. Pour onto an oiled baking tray and allow to cool.

Pour 300 ml (½ pint) of the cream into a saucepan. Scrape the seeds out of the vanilla pod and add them to the cream. Slowly bring to the boil. Meanwhile, in a bowl whisk the egg yolks with 50 g (2 oz) sugar until creamy. Pour on the hot cream, whisking all the time. Return to the pan and stir over a low heat until thick enough to coat the back of the spoon. Strain the custard into a bowl and cover the surface closely with a piece of buttered greaseproof paper to prevent a skin forming. Allow to cool, then chill for 1 hour.

Whisk 100 ml (3½ fl oz) cream and the liqueur into the chilled custard base. Purée the apricots in a blender or food processor and divide between 4 ramekins. Spoon the custard mixture over the apricot purée, cover and place in the freezer for 1 hour.

Break up the praline and place in the food processor. Work until the mixture resembles sugar. Sprinkle evenly over the mousses and place under a preheated hot grill for 1 minute. Allow to cool, then refrigerate for 30 minutes before serving.

Note: Preserved apricots in Amaretto, sold in jars, are available from delicatessens and large supermarkets.

REGIONAL HEATS
THE SOUTH EAST
HELEN WELLER • CAROL BARTLETT • MARC HADLEY

CAROL BARTLETT'S MENU

STARTER
*Baked Wild Mushrooms with Garlic and Cheese, served
on a Bread Croûte*

MAIN COURSE
*Rack of Lamb with Oranges and Cointreau
Potato and Carrot Rösti
Filo Boats with Leek Purée*
"THERE'S A LOT GOING ON, BUT EVERYTHING IS RELEVANT" PRUE LEITH

DESSERT
*Poached Pears in Sauternes Sauce with Almonds
and Praline*
"A TOP CLASS DISH" LOYD

Carol Bartlett, from Fordingbridge in Hampshire, is a
marketing manager for a veterinary pharmaceutical
company. She is also the secretary to the committee
responsible for the celebrated annual agricultural show.
Carol's personal interest in animals is directed towards
racing whippets which she breeds and trains.

BAKED WILD MUSHROOMS WITH GARLIC AND CHEESE

Use a mixture of wild and cultivated mushrooms – such as ceps, chanterelles, oyster mushrooms and cup mushrooms. If wild mushrooms are unavailable, use a mixture of cultivated ones, including flat mushrooms.

400 g (14 oz) mixed mushrooms
2 cloves garlic, crushed
75 g (3 oz) butter, melted
45 ml (3 tbsp) chopped parsley
90 ml (6 tbsp) double cream
salt and freshly ground black pepper
50 g (2 oz) Emmental cheese, grated

Bread Croûtes:
4 slices of bread
25 g (1 oz) butter
30 ml (2 tbsp) oil
1 clove garlic, crushed
30 ml (2 tbsp) chopped parsley

Slice the mushrooms and place in a large buttered dish. Add the garlic to the melted butter and pour over the mushrooms. Mix together the parsley, cream and salt and pepper, then pour over the mushrooms. Bake in a preheated oven at 200°C (400°F) mark 6 for 15 minutes.

Meanwhile prepare the bread croûtes. Cut 4 rounds, 6 cm (2½ inches) in diameter, from the slices of bread. Heat the butter and oil in a frying pan with the garlic. Add the bread rounds and fry on both sides until crisp and golden. Drain on kitchen paper, then roll the edge of each croûte first in the oil and butter, then in chopped parsley to coat evenly.

Stir the cooked mushrooms thoroughly, then divide between 4 shallow ovenproof serving dishes. Sprinkle with a little cheese, then return to the oven for a few minutes until the cheese is melted. Sprinkle with chopped parsley and serve immediately, with the croûtes.

FILO BOATS WITH LEEK PURÉE

3 sheets of filo pastry
50 g (2 oz) butter, melted

Leek Purée:
350 g (12 oz) leeks
50 g (2 oz) butter
30 ml (2 tbsp) well-flavoured stock
15 ml (1 tbsp) chopped parsley
salt and freshly ground black pepper

To Garnish:
chives

Line 12 small boat-shaped moulds with 3 layers of filo pastry, cutting the pastry to fit and brushing each layer liberally with melted butter. Bake in a preheated oven at 190-200°C (375-400°F) mark 5-6 for 5-7 minutes until golden.

To make the leek purée, trim the leeks, leaving most of the green part attached, then slice finely. Heat the butter and stock in a pan, then add the leeks. Cook over a low heat until the leeks are tender but not coloured. Add the parsley, then purée the mixture in a food processor or blender until smooth. Season with salt and pepper to taste.

Place a little leek purée in each filo boat and garnish with chives. Serve three filo boats per person.

Note: Any leftover leek purée can be frozen for future use.

RACK OF LAMB WITH ORANGES AND COINTREAU

2 best ends of lamb, each with 6 cutlets
1 clove garlic, crushed
15 ml (1 tbsp) melted butter
juice of ½ orange
30 ml (2 tbsp) soft dark brown sugar

Sauce:
50 g (2 oz) butter (approximately)
2 shallots, chopped
1 clove garlic, crushed
*300 ml (½ pint) well-flavoured lamb or beef
  stock*
175 ml (6 fl oz) red wine
juice of 1 orange
salt and freshly ground black pepper
30 ml (2 tbsp) Cointreau
5 ml (1 tsp) brown sugar (optional)

To Garnish:
1 orange

Trim the lamb of excess fat, then rub all over with the garlic and brush with melted butter. Place, fat side uppermost, in a roasting tin and sprinkle with the orange juice, then the brown sugar.

To prepare the garnish, finely pare the rind from the orange, making sure there is no pith, then cut the rind into julienne strips. Blanch these in boiling water for 1 minute then refresh with cold water; drain. Peel and segment the orange, discarding all white pith and pips.

To make the sauce, melt the butter in a pan and sauté the shallots with the garlic until soft but not coloured. Add the stock and reduce by half. Add the red wine and again reduce by half. Finally add the orange juice, then strain into a clean pan and simmer gently for 1 minute. Season with salt and pepper. Add the Cointreau, then taste and adjust the seasoning, adding a little sugar if necessary.

Cook the lamb in a preheated oven at 220°C (425°F) mark 7 for 30 minutes, until tender but still pink inside. Remove from the oven and leave to rest in a warm place for 5-10 minutes. Pour any meat juices from the tin into the sauce. Reheat the sauce and whisk in a small knob of butter to add gloss if necessary.

Divide the lamb into cutlets and place 3 cutlets on each warmed plate with the bones towards the centre, and the eye of the meat to the outside. Pour the sauce around the meat and garnish with the orange segments and julienne strips.

POTATO AND CARROT RÖSTI

350 g (12 oz) potatoes
salt and freshly ground black pepper
225 g (8 oz) carrots, coarsely grated
1 clove garlic, crushed
*5 ml (1 tsp) roasted coriander seeds, ground
  (optional)*
15 ml (1 tbsp) oil
50 g (2 oz) butter

Parboil the potatoes in their skins in boiling salted water for 10 minutes. Carefully peel while still warm. Allow to cool, then grate coarsely and turn into a bowl. Add the carrots, garlic, coriander if using, and seasoning.

Heat the oil and butter in a large heavy-based pan. Place four 5-7.5 cm (2-3 inch) plain pastry cutters or crumpet rings in the pan. Carefully spoon the rösti mixture into the rings, pressing down until well compacted.

Lower the heat and cook for about 10 minutes until golden brown underneath. Carefully remove the rings, turn the rösti and cook the other side until golden brown. Serve with the lamb.

POACHED PEARS IN SAUTERNES SAUCE WITH ALMONDS AND PRALINE

4 ripe firm Comice pears
16 small ratafia biscuits
1 glass Sauternes

Praline:
75 g (3 oz) granulated sugar
50 g (2 oz) whole almonds (with skins on)

Syrup:
125 g (4 oz) sugar
120 ml (4 fl oz) Sauternes

Sauternes Sauce:
4 egg yolks
50 g (2 oz) granulated sugar
60 ml (2 fl oz) Sauternes
30-45 ml (1 heaped tbsp) crème fraîche

To Finish:
icing sugar, for dusting
30 ml (2 tbsp) flaked almonds
mint leaves, to decorate

First prepare the praline. Place the sugar and almonds in a heavy-based pan over a low heat. Heat, without stirring, until the sugar is melted, golden brown and forms a coating on the almonds. Pour onto an oiled slab or baking sheet and leave to cool. When completely cold, grind to a powder in a blender or food processor.

Meanwhile to make the syrup, dissolve the sugar in 150 ml (¼ pint) water in a heavy-based pan over a low heat. Add the Sauternes. Peel the pears, add them to the syrup and poach gently for about 20 minutes, or until tender. Remove the pears from the syrup and allow to cool.

Soak the ratafias in Sauternes, then place four in each of 4 ovenproof gratin dishes. Halve each pear lengthways and remove the cores. Slice almost through to the stalk end, fan out and arrange on top of the ratafias.

To make the Sauternes sauce, whisk together the egg yolks and sugar in a bowl over a pan of simmering water until the mixture is pale golden and thick. Whisk in the Sauternes, then remove the bowl from the pan. Allow to cool, then fold in the crème fraîche.

Pour the sauce over the pears, sprinkle each serving with 20-25 ml (1½ tbsp) praline. Dust with icing sugar and sprinkle with flaked almonds. Place under a preheated grill for about 1 minute until lightly browned. Decorate with mint leaves and serve immediately.

REGIONAL HEATS
THE SOUTH EAST
HELEN WELLER • CAROL BARTLETT • MARC HADLEY

MARC HADLEY'S MENU

STARTER
Surfin' Prawns

MAIN COURSE
Pan-fried Beef Medallions in a Curry and Port Sauce
"IT WAS AWFULLY GOOD – THE BEEF WITH THE CURRY" LOYD

Ginger and Yogurt Relish
Glazed Carrots
French Beans
Potatoes

DESSERT
Pears Baked in a Juniper and Vanilla Sauce
"I THOUGHT THE JUNIPER WITH THE PEAR WAS LOVELY... A MOST
BEAUTIFUL DISH" MAX HASTINGS

Marc Hadley comes from Horsham in West Sussex. As an environmental auditor, Marc searches out pollution on commercial and industrial sites and develops techniques to remove it. He has a penchant for fast cars, and many a Sunday morning is spent at Goodwood putting his Porsche through its high speed paces!

SURFIN' PRAWNS

6-8 shallots
75 g (3 oz) butter
15 ml (1 tbsp) fresh green peppercorns
  (see note)
salt and freshly ground black pepper
175 g (6 oz) monkfish fillet, membrane
  removed
225 g (8 oz) raw prawns
120 ml (4 fl oz) white wine
1 bunch of dill sprigs
finely grated rind and juice of ½ lemon, or
  to taste
4 egg whites
4 cooked Dublin Bay prawns (in shell)

Dice the shallots very finely. Melt the butter in a frying pan, add the shallots and green peppercorns and fry gently until softened. Season to taste.

Meanwhile cut the monkfish into small pieces. Shell the prawns and add to the pan with the monkfish. Cook gently for 5-10 minutes. Using a slotted spoon, transfer the fish, prawns, shallots and peppercorns to 4 ramekins.

Add the wine to the liquid remaining in the pan. Strip the leaves from the dill sprigs and set aside; finely chop the stalks and add to the pan. Bring to the boil and reduce by half over a high heat. Lower the heat and add the lemon rind and juice, then pour into the ramekins.

Finely chop the dill leaves. Whisk the egg whites until stiff, then fold in the dill leaves. Spoon over the mixture in the ramekins. Separate the heads and tails of the Dublin Bay prawns and arrange on top. Cook in a preheated oven at 200°C (400°F) mark 6 for about 5 minutes until the egg white is cooked through and crisp. Serve immediately.

Note: If fresh green peppercorns are unavailable substitute green peppercorns in brine, well drained.

PAN-FRIED BEEF MEDALLIONS IN A CURRY AND PORT SAUCE

For this recipe you will need to buy a piece of beef cut from the whole fillet, suitable for slicing into small medallions, 4-5 cm (1½ -2 inches) in diameter.

450 g 1 lb) fillet steak
10 ml (2 tsp) coriander seeds, freshly ground
10 ml (2 tsp) turmeric
salt and freshly ground black pepper
75 g (3 oz) butter
10 shallots, finely chopped
5 ml (1 tsp) cumin seeds
pinch of asafoetida powder
275 ml (9 fl oz) port

Slice the beef into thin medallions. Mix the ground coriander with the turmeric and salt and pepper and use to coat the medallions; set aside.

Heat the butter in a frying pan until foaming but not brown. Add the shallots, cumin seeds and asafoetida and fry, stirring, over a moderate heat for 5-10 minutes.

Using a slotted spoon, transfer the shallots to a plate, then increase the heat and quickly fry the beef medallions for 1-2 minutes each side until browned; do not overcook. Transfer the medallions to a warmed serving dish. Return the shallots to the pan, add the port and bring to the boil. Reduce the sauce by half, then pour over the medallions and serve at once, with the ginger and yogurt relish and vegetable accompaniments.

GINGER AND YOGURT RELISH

50 g (2 oz) fresh root ginger, peeled
4 cloves garlic
2-3 large green chillies
30 ml (2 tbsp) desiccated coconut
5 ml (1 tsp) caster sugar
2.5-5 ml (½-1 tsp) salt
150-175 ml (5-6 fl oz) yogurt

Dressing:
50 g (2 oz) ghee
12 curry leaves
12 tiny dried red chillies
5 ml (1 tsp) mustard seeds

Roughly chop the ginger and place in a food processor with the garlic. Halve and deseed the chillies and add to the processor bowl with the coconut, sugar and salt. Work to a fine paste. Fold into the yogurt and spoon the relish onto the serving plates.

To make the dressing, heat the ghee in a heavy-based pan until hot. Add the curry leaves, red chillies and mustard seeds, and fry until the seeds begin to pop. Spoon a little of the seed and oil mixture onto the relish, arranging the curry leaves and chillies to garnish.

PEARS BAKED IN A JUNIPER AND VANILLA SAUCE

50 g (2 oz) butter, unsalted
15 ml (1 tbsp) dried juniper berries (see note)
30 ml (2 tbsp) soft brown sugar
6 ripe firm pears
350 ml (12 fl oz) port
2 vanilla pods

Melt the butter in a frying pan, add the dried juniper berries and fry gently for 2-3 minutes. Add the brown sugar and allow to dissolve over a low heat.

Meanwhile peel the pears leaving the stalks on; halve and remove the cores. Place the pear halves in the pan with the juniper berries and fry gently for 5-10 minutes until slightly browned. Add half of the port and turn the pears frequently until they start to take up the port.

Using a slotted spoon, transfer the pear halves to a lightly greased baking dish. Add the remaining port to the pan with the vanilla pods and bring to the boil, then reduce the sauce by one third. Pour over the pears in the baking dish, cover with a lid and cook in a preheated oven at 180°C (350°F) mark 4 for about 1 hour until tender, basting the pears at regular intervals with the sauce.

Arrange the pears on serving plates, pour over the sauce and serve immediately, with cream.

Note: To improve the flavour of the dried juniper berries, soak them in gin overnight before use.

REGIONAL HEATS

SCOTLAND

BETSY ANDERSON • MICHAEL BAXTER • JONATHAN CASTLE

WINNER

BETSY ANDERSON'S MENU

STARTER

Oysters au Gratin

"THE OYSTERS GAVE A GREAT TANG OF THE SEA THE MOMENT
YOU TOOK A TASTE. IT WAS TERRIFIC" MARTYN LEWIS

MAIN COURSE

Pan-fried Fillet of Salmon with a Tomato and Basil Vinaigrette
Baby Vegetables en Papilotte

DESSERT

Blueberry Shortcake with a Fruit Coulis

"I THOUGHT BETSY'S PUDDING WAS ABSOLUTELY
DELICIOUS" LESLIE FORBES

Betsy Anderson comes from East Calder in West Lothian. Originally trained as a lawyer, she is now an overseas investment dealer with an Edinburgh firm of fund managers. Betsy and her husband Steven are enthusiastic weekend campers, and have pitched their tent all over Scotland. Back at home, Betsy's creative energy is evident in her stencilling in the new study.

OYSTERS AU GRATIN

12 oysters, scrubbed clean
100 ml (3½ fl oz) dry white wine
1 carrot, sliced
1 stick celery, sliced
15 ml (1 tbsp) lemon juice
100 ml (3½ fl oz) single cream
2 egg yolks
salt and freshly ground black pepper
30 ml (2 tbsp) grated mozzarella cheese

To Serve:
45 ml (3 tbsp) rock salt
lemon wedges
herb sprigs

Put the oysters on a baking tray and place in a preheated oven at 180°C (350°F) mark 4 for 1-2 minutes until they open. Remove the oysters from their shells, reserving the juices. Clean out the empty shells.

Place the white wine, carrot, celery, lemon juice and reserved oyster juice in a saucepan and cook for 5 minutes until the vegetables are tender and the stock is reduced. Strain the stock, discarding the vegetables (they are simply used to add flavour).

Return the oysters to their shells and place in a baking dish. In a bowl, whisk the cream and egg yolks together, then pour on the stock, stirring. Return to the pan and cook gently over a low heat, stirring constantly, until slightly thickened. Season with salt and pepper to taste, then pour the sauce evenly over the oysters.

Sprinkle with the grated cheese and place under a preheated grill until melted and lightly browned. Serve the oysters, three per person, each resting on a bed of rock salt. Garnish with lemon wedges and herb sprigs.

PAN-FRIED FILLET OF SALMON WITH A TOMATO AND BASIL VINAIGRETTE

15 ml (1 tbsp) butter
5 ml (1 tsp) chopped herbs
5 ml (1 tsp) crushed or finely chopped garlic
4 Scottish salmon fillets, skinned

Vinaigrette:
175 ml (6 fl oz) olive oil
60 ml (4 tbsp) cider vinegar
5 ml (1 tsp) honey
1 clove garlic, crushed
15 ml (1 tbsp) finely chopped tomato flesh
15 ml (1 tbsp) chopped basil
salt and freshly ground black pepper

To Garnish:
lemon wedges
herb sprigs

First make the vinaigrette. Place all the ingredients in a screw-topped jar and shake well. Season with salt and pepper.

Melt the butter in a frying pan, add the herbs and garlic, then add the salmon fillets and cook over a high heat for about 10-15 seconds each side to seal. Turn the heat down to medium and cook for 6-8 minutes, until the salmon is just cooked and flakes easily when tested with a fork.

Place one salmon fillet in the middle of each warmed serving plate. Give the vinaigrette a good shake and spoon over the salmon. Garnish with lemon and basil to serve.

Note: The vinaigrette can be stored for up to 4 weeks in a cool place. Shake vigorously before use.

BABY VEGETABLES EN PAPILOTTE

For the papilottes you will need 4 sheets of greaseproof paper and ideally 8 wooden clothes pegs, or heat-resistant plastic clips.

12 baby carrots
8 cauliflower florets
12 baby corn cobs
12 mangetouts
8 broccoli florets
salt and freshly ground black pepper
5 bouquet garnis, tied with string

Herb Butter:
125 g (4 oz) butter, softened
10-15 ml (2-3 tsp) herbs
5-10 ml (1-2 tsp) lemon juice

First make the herb butter. Put the butter, herbs and lemon juice in a bowl and mix well. Season with salt and pepper to taste. Set aside.

Bring a large pan of water to the boil. Add the carrots and cauliflower and par-boil for about 3 minutes, then remove with a slotted spoon.

Place a bamboo steamer over the pan of boiling water and place all of the vegetables in the steamer, together with one of the herb bouquets. Cover and steam the vegetables for 6 minutes. Remove the steamer from the heat.

Distribute the vegetables evenly between 4 buttered sheets of grease-proof paper, placing them in the centre of the paper. Sprinkle with a little salt and top each portion with a spoonful of the herb butter. Bring the two ends of the paper together, then roll down leaving enough space for air to circulate. Twist the two open ends and secure with wooden clothes pegs. Place in a microwave oven and cook on HIGH for 30 seconds.

Serve the vegetables in their paper packets. Garnish each serving with a bouquet of herbs.

Note: Reheating the vegetables by microwave ensures that they retain their bright colours. Alternatively you could return to the steamer to heat through.

BLUEBERRY SHORTCAKE WITH A FRUIT COULIS

Make sure the oven is at the correct temperature before you put the shortbread rounds in to cook.

Blueberry Cream:
200 g (7 oz) blueberries
300 ml (½ pint) whipping cream
50 g (2 oz) icing sugar, sifted

Fruit Coulis:
50 g (2 oz) blueberries
50 g (2 oz) raspberries
30 ml (2 tbsp) icing sugar, sifted
15 ml (1 tbsp) drambuie

Shortbread Biscuits:
175 g (6 oz) plain flour
25 g (1 oz) caster sugar
75 g (3 oz) butter
30 ml (2 tbsp) milk

To Decorate:
icing sugar, for dusting
a little single cream
few raspberries and blueberries

To make the blueberry cream, place the blueberries in a food processor and work to a purée, then sieve to remove the seeds. Put the whipping cream in the food processor and process until it forms firm peaks; do not overwork. Turn into a bowl and fold in the icing sugar and blueberry purée until evenly blended. Cover and place in the refrigerator to chill and 'firm up' the mixture.

To make the fruit coulis, purée the blueberries and raspberries in the food processor and pass through a sieve twice to remove all the seeds. Add the icing sugar and drambuie and stir until the sugar has dissolved and the coulis has a smooth consistency. Cover and chill in the refrigerator until required.

To make the shortbread biscuits, sift the flour into the processor and add the sugar, butter and milk. Process briefly until the mixture forms a smooth dough; the mixture must not be too 'short' otherwise it will crumble when rolled out thinly.

Roll out the dough very thinly on a floured surface. Using a 6 cm (2½ inch) pastry cutter, cut out 12 biscuits. Place on a lightly greased baking tray and bake in the top of a preheated oven at 180°C (350°F) mark 4 for 8-10 minutes or until crisp and golden. Remove from the oven and carefully transfer to a wire rack to cool.

To assemble the shortcakes, place a biscuit in the centre of each serving plate. Spoon on some of the blueberry cream, then cover with another biscuit. Add another spoonful of blueberry cream and finally top with a biscuit. Sprinkle with icing sugar. Pour some of the fruit coulis around each shortcake to make a pool. Spoon tiny blobs of single cream on to the coulis and draw a cocktail stick through the cream to make a feathered design. Top with a few raspberries and blueberries.

REGIONAL HEATS

SCOTLAND

BETSY ANDERSON • MICHAEL BAXTER • JONATHAN CASTLE

MICHAEL BAXTER'S MENU

STARTER

Salmon Tartare with Crème Fraîche and Dill Vinaigrette

MAIN COURSE

*Roast Duck Breast with a Wild Mushroom Sauce, served
with Duck Mousse Filo Parcels
Potato and Spinach Galettes*

DESSERT

Bread and Butter Pudding with Rum and Prunes

"I LOVED THE RUM WITH THE BREAD AND BUTTER
PUDDING" LESLIE FORBES

"IN TERMS OF OVERALL BALANCE, THE MENU WAS VERY
GOOD" MARTYN LEWIS

Michael Baxter lives in Elgin in Moray. As a director of the family food business, Michael is responsible for selling the familiar miniature jars of preserves worldwide. His hobbies befit a Scottish gentleman: the occasional round of golf, and fishing for salmon in the nearby river Spey.

SALMON TARTARE WITH CRÈME FRAÎCHE AND DILL VINAIGRETTE

Gravad Lax is lightly salted salmon
flavoured with dill; a Swedish speciality, it is
widely available in this country. You will
find it easier to dice and mix the fish if it is
partially frozen first.

225 g (8 oz) skinned salmon fillets
125 g (4 oz) gravad lax
125 g (4 oz) clarified butter
1 shallot, finely diced
1 clove garlic, halved
5 ml (1 tsp) chopped dill
lemon juice, to taste
salt and freshly ground black pepper

Dill Vinaigrette:
60 ml (4 tbsp) olive oil
15 ml (1 tbsp) white wine vinegar
2.5 ml (½ tsp) chopped dill
30 ml (2 tbsp) finely diced tomato flesh

To Serve:
60 ml (4 tbsp) crème fraîche

Finely dice the salmon and gravad lax
and mix well.

Heat the clarified butter in a pan and
sauté the shallot and garlic for 1 minute,
then discard the garlic. Add the butter
mixture to the salmon together with the
dill and lemon juice to taste. Season with
salt and pepper to taste. Mix well and
chill in the refrigerator until required.

Whisk together the ingredients for the
vinaigrette, or shake vigorously in a
screw-topped jar, adding salt and
pepper to taste.

To serve, spoon the dill vinaigrette on
to individual serving plates. Form the
salmon tartare into quenelles, using two
moistened tablespoons to shape the
ovals. Position 3 quenelles on each plate
and spoon some crème fraîche into the
middle. Serve at once.

Clarified Butter: This can be heated to a
much higher temperature than ordinary
butter without burning. To prepare clarified butter, melt the butter in a pan over
a low heat, then skim the froth from the
surface. Remove from the heat and
allow to stand until the sediment settles
on the bottom of the pan. Carefully pour
the clarified butter into a clean bowl,
leaving the sediment behind.

ROAST DUCK BREAST WITH A WILD MUSHROOM SAUCE

This main course is served with a delicate garnish of Duck Mousse Filo Parcels (see overleaf).

2 Greshingham ducks
clear honey, for brushing
rock salt, for sprinkling
15 ml (1 tbsp) clarified butter

Wild Mushroom Sauce:

25 g (1 oz) dried chanterelles
15 ml (1 tbsp) clarified butter
30 ml (2 tbsp) each of diced shallot, carrot
  and celery
2 cloves garlic, halved
pinch of dried thyme
½ bay leaf
10 ml (2 tsp) tomato purée
75 ml (3 oz) madeira
175 ml (6 fl oz) dry white wine
900 ml (1½ pints) chicken stock
salt and freshly ground white pepper

Carefully remove the duck breasts. Brush the duck breast skin with honey, then sprinkle with rock salt. Skin and bone the legs. Chop up 175 g (6 oz) leg meat and set aside for the mousse.

To prepare the sauce, soak the chanterelles in warm water to cover for 30 minutes. Meanwhile, heat 15 ml (1 tbsp) clarified butter in a large heavy-based pan and brown the duck bones in the butter. Add the diced vegetables and garlic, and sauté for 2-3 minutes. Stir in the herbs and tomato purée. Deglaze the pan with the madeira, stirring to scrape up the sediment. Add the wine and reduce by half. Add the stock and boil steadily to reduce by half, skimming frequently.

Strain the sauce through a fine sieve into a clean pan and add the mushrooms. Simmer for 5 minutes, then transfer to a blender or food processor and work until smooth. Return to the pan and boil for 15 minutes. Pass through a sieve lined with a double layer of muslin into a clean pan and reduce to a coating consistency. Season with salt and pepper to taste; keep warm.

Heat 15 ml (1 tbsp) clarified butter in a heavy-based pan and fry the duck breasts, skin side down, for 5 minutes. Turn and cook the other side until browned. Place, skin-side up, in a roasting tin and cook in a preheated oven at 190°C (375°F) mark 5 for 5 minutes. Cover and leave to rest in a warm place for 5 minutes.

Carve the duck breasts and arrange on warmed serving plates. Spoon over the sauce and arrange a duck mousse filo parcel on each plate. Serve with potato and spinach galettes.

DUCK MOUSSE FILO PARCELS

few dried chanterelles
45 ml (3 tbsp) clarified butter, melted
2 shallots, finely chopped
pinch of dried thyme
1 clove garlic, skinned
175 g (6 oz) duck leg meat, trimmed of
  sinew and skin
250 ml (8 fl oz) double cream
1 egg, size 3, beaten
salt and freshly ground black pepper
1 packet of filo pastry
4 long strips of leek, blanched

Soak the chanterelles in warm water to cover for 1 hour; drain and chop finely. Heat 15 ml (1 tbsp) clarified butter in a pan. Add the chanterelles, shallots, thyme and whole garlic clove and sauté gently for 3 minutes. Discard the garlic and drain off any liquid. Place in a bowl, cover and chill in the refrigerator.

Put the duck meat in a food processor and chop finely. Add the cream, egg and seasoning and work until smooth. Transfer to a bowl, cover and chill thoroughly.

Cut twelve 10 cm (4 inch) squares of filo pastry and brush liberally with melted butter. Layer the filo squares in threes, to give 4 piles. Place a spoonful of chilled mousse in the middle of each filo pile, together with a spoonful of the chilled mushroom mixture. Draw up the corners of the filo pastry over the filling and pinch together to seal, forming small parcels. Tie a blanched leek strip around the top of each one. Cook in a preheated oven at 190°C (375°F) mark 5 for 10-15 minutes until crisp and golden.

POTATO AND SPINACH GALETTES

175 g (6 oz) young spinach leaves
salt and freshly ground white pepper
freshly grated nutmeg, to taste
2 baking potatoes
120 ml (8 tbsp) clarified butter

Chop the spinach leaves and blanch briefly in boiling salted water until just wilted. Refresh in cold water. Drain thoroughly and pat dry with kitchen paper. Season lightly with nutmeg.

Peel the potatoes and grate coarsely into long strips if possible. Dry thoroughly with a cloth or kitchen paper, then place in a bowl. Add 60 ml (4 tbsp) clarified butter and mix well. Season with salt and pepper.

Grease four 10 cm (4 inch) muffin rings. Press half of the grated potato into the rings, then cover with the spinach. Top with the remaining potato and press down.

Heat the remaining clarified butter in a heavy-based pan and carefully place the potato galettes in the pan. Cook over a moderate heat until crisp and brown underneath. Run a knife around the rings to loosen them, then remove. Turn the galettes over and cook until the other side is crisp and brown. Drain on kitchen paper. Serve at once.

Note: These galettes can be prepared ahead if necessary, and reheated in a moderate oven before serving.

BREAD AND BUTTER PUDDING WITH RUM AND PRUNES

6 slices buttered bread
butter, for spreading
350 ml (12 fl oz) single cream
60 ml (4 tbsp) dark rum
few drops of vanilla essence
6 egg yolks
50 g (2 oz) caster sugar
50 g (2 oz) no-soak prunes, stoned and diced

Raspberry Coulis:
175 g (6 oz) raspberries
10 ml (2 tsp) icing sugar
10 ml (2 tsp) lemon juice
10 ml (2 tsp) orange juice

Rum Sabayon:
6 egg yolks
50 g (2 oz) caster sugar
60 ml (4 tbsp) rum
120 ml (4 fl oz) whipping cream, lightly
  whipped

Butter the bread, discard the crusts, then cut into 2.5 cm (1 inch) squares.

Heat the cream, rum and vanilla in a saucepan to just below boiling point, then remove from the heat. In a bowl, beat the egg yolks and sugar together until pale then gradually add the cream, whisking all the time. Strain through a fine sieve.

Layer the bread and prunes in 4 buttered ramekins. Pour in the cream to saturate the bread. Leave to stand for about 30 minutes.

Place the ramekins in a bain-marie (or roasting tin containing enough hot water to come halfway up the sides of the ramekins). Bake in a preheated oven at 180°C (350°F) mark 4 for 35-40 minutes.

Meanwhile to make the raspberry coulis, purée the raspberries with the icing sugar and lemon and orange juices in a blender or food processor. Pass through a sieve to remove the seeds.

To make the rum sabayon, put the egg yolks, sugar and rum in a large heat-proof bowl over a pan of hot water and whisk until thick and creamy. Remove from the pan and whisk until cool; then fold in the whipped cream.

To serve, turn the bread and butter puddings out of the ramekins and place on individual serving plates with a portion of the rum sabayon. Serve accompanied by the raspberry coulis.

Regional Heats

Scotland

Betsy Anderson • Michael Baxter • Jonathan Castle

Jonathan Castle's Menu

Starter

Truckle of Woodland Mushrooms, scented with Whisky

"The memory of those terrific wild mushrooms will
last a long time" Martyn Lewis

Main Course

Tempura of Monkfish with a Bitter Orange Sauce
Timbales of White and Wild Rice
Broccoli Steamed with Mirin

Dessert

Warm Bramble Soufflés, with Heather Honey Cream

"I did think the Bramble Soufflé was very good" Loyd

Jonathan Castle moved from Sidcup in Kent to Edinburgh, where he works as a freelance copywriter. As a keen sailor and erstwhile boatbuilder he enjoys helping out on a friend's forty year old wooden yacht in his spare time. Jonathan also enjoys a visit to the malt whisky distillery to sample the local vintages.

TRUCKLE OF WOODLAND MUSHROOMS, SCENTED WITH WHISKY

Select your wild mushrooms according to the season. Use ceps, morels, hedgehog mushrooms, field mushrooms, etc. Alternatively, if wild mushrooms are unavailable, use 350 g (12 oz) button mushrooms and 25 g (1 oz) each of dried ceps and morels. Soak dried mushrooms in boiling water to cover for 30 minutes. Drain and gently squeeze dry, then use as fresh ones.

450 g (1 lb) mixed wild mushrooms
50 g (2 oz) Parma knuckle
1 clove garlic
50 g (2 oz) unsalted butter
50 ml (2 fl oz) good whisky
handful of chopped parsley
salt and freshly ground black pepper
15-30 ml (1-2 tbsp) double cream (optional)

To Serve:
warm focaccia or French bread
selection of salad leaves
vinaigrette (made with balsamic vinegar)

Trim, clean and coarsely slice the mushrooms. Roughly chop the Parma ham. Finely chop half of the garlic clove. Finely slice the other half; set aside.

Heat the butter in a large sauté pan, add the chopped garlic and cook gently until golden. Add the chopped Parma ham. Add the firm-fleshed mushroom varieties to the pan first, and sauté gently for a few minutes, then add the remaining mushrooms and sliced garlic and sauté briefly.

Increase the heat and add the whisky to the pan. Allow to bubble until all excess liquid has evaporated. Stir in a good handful of chopped parsley and add seasoning to taste. For a richer sauce, stir in the cream and heat through just before serving.

Serve on a bed of warm focaccia or French bread with a salad of seasonal leaves dressed with a little balsamic vinaigrette.

Note: Parma knuckle is an inexpensive way of buying the prized ham. If unobtainable, use Parma ham or any other similar raw cured ham.

TEMPURA OF MONKFISH WITH A BITTER ORANGE SAUCE

675 g (1½ lb) monkfish tail (bone in)
salt and freshly ground black pepper
safflower oil, for deep-frying

Tempura Batter:
50 g (2 oz) plain flour
15 g (½ oz) cornflour
2.5 ml (½ tsp) salt
150-175 ml (5-6 fl oz) cold water

Bitter Orange Sauce:
2 organic oranges
1 Seville orange
1 pink grapefruit
150 ml (¼ pint) dry sherry
150 ml (¼ pint) fish stock (approximately)
brown sugar, to taste (optional)
soy sauce, to taste (optional)
25 g (1 oz) unsalted butter, chilled and diced

First prepare the batter. Sift both flours into a bowl with the salt. Beat in the water, a little at a time, until the batter is the consistency of single cream. Chill in the refrigerator for 30 minutes.

Meanwhile, trim the monkfish. Remove the bone and tough outer membrane, then cut into medallions, about 2.5 cm (1 inch) across and 1 cm (½ inch) thick. Season with salt and pepper, then chill.

To make the sauce, squeeze the juice from the oranges and grapefruit and mix together; you should have about 300 ml (½ pint). Bring the sherry to the boil in a saucepan and reduce by half. Add the citrus juice and reduce again by half. Add about 150 ml (¼ pint) fish stock (depending how strong and salty it is). Reduce slightly until you have a rich, tart sauce. If it is too tart, add a little sugar; if too fruity, add a little soy sauce to bring out the fish flavour. When ready to serve, whisk in the butter a piece at a time, to add gloss.

Heat the oil in a wok or deep-fryer until very hot. Cook the monkfish in small batches: dip a few medallions into the chilled batter, then quickly fry in the oil for about 2 minutes until crisp and golden brown. Drain on kitchen paper; keep warm while cooking the remainder. Serve immediately, with the sauce.

TIMBALES OF WHITE AND WILD RICE

50 g (2 oz) wild rice
225 g (8 oz) basmati rice
4 cardamom pods
50 ml (2 fl oz) fish stock (approximately)

Put the wild rice in a pan of cold salted water, bring to the boil and simmer for 20 minutes. Add the basmati rice, bring back to the boil and simmer for 10 minutes. Rinse with boiling water; drain.

Butter 4 individual moulds, crush a cardamom pod into each one, then pack with rice. To each mould, add 5-10 ml (1-2 tsp) fish stock to moisten. Place the moulds in a roasting tin containing enough warm water to come halfway up the sides. Cover with foil and place in the oven at 160°C (325°F) mark 3 for about 5 minutes to set. Turn out onto warmed plates to serve.

BROCCOLI STEAMED WITH MIRIN

450 g (1 lb) broccoli
120 ml (4 fl oz) mirin
strips of candied lemon peel, to garnish

Divide the broccoli into small florets. Place in the top of a steamer over a pan of boiling water to which the mirin has been added. Cover and steam for 3-4 minutes until the broccoli is cooked but retains its colour and 'bite'. Serve garnished with candied lemon peel.

Vanilla Pears with an Almond Filling and Chocolate Sauce
RICHARD KUCH'S DESSERT (SEMI-FINAL)

Turban of Sole and Salmon with a Watercress Sauce
TONY DAVIS' MAIN COURSE (SEMI-FINAL)

WARM BRAMBLE SOUFFLÉS, WITH HEATHER HONEY CREAM

For this dessert I use flavourful wild Scottish brambles. To make vanilla sugar, simply leave one or two vanilla pods in a jar of caster sugar to impart flavour and fragrance. You may need to adjust the quantity of sugar according to the sweetness of the fruit.

25 g (1 oz) unsalted butter
25 g (1 oz) self-raising flour
150 ml (¼ pint) milk
125 g (4 oz) vanilla sugar (approximately)
    or caster sugar and a few drops of
    vanilla essence
450 g (1 lb) blackberries
squeeze of lemon juice, or to taste
4 eggs, size 1, separated
icing sugar, for dusting

Heather Honey Cream:
120 ml (4 fl oz) single cream
60 ml (2 fl oz) Greek yogurt
5 ml (1 tsp) heather-flavoured honey
    (approximately)

Melt the butter in a saucepan. Add the flour and cook, stirring, for 1 minute. Remove from the heat and gradually blend in the milk. Stir in half of the sugar (and vanilla essence if using). Cook, stirring, for 2 minutes, then remove from the heat.

Set aside 8-12 blackberries; put the rest into a heavy-based pan with the remaining sugar and lemon juice. Cover and cook gently for about 5 minutes until softened, then strain through a nylon sieve. Reserve 15-30 ml (1-2 tbsp) fruit pureé for decoration; stir the rest into the sauce.

Whisk the egg whites in a spotlessly clean bowl until they form soft peaks. Beat the egg yolks together, then stir into the flavoured sauce. Gently whisk in a quarter of the whisked egg white, then lightly fold in the rest, using a spatula.

Butter 4 ramekin dishes, each 9 cm (3½ inches) in diameter and sprinkle lightly with sugar. Half-fill the dishes with soufflé mixture, arrange the reserved blackberries on top and cover with the remaining mixture. Dust the tops with icing sugar and place in a roasting tin. Add enough boiling water to the tin to come halfway up the sides of the dishes. Bake in a preheated oven at 180°C (350°F) mark 4 for about 12 minutes until risen and set. Remove from the roasting tin and allow to cool.

Meanwhile to make the heather honey cream, simply combine the cream and yogurt with honey to taste, stirring until smooth.

To serve, carefully turn the soufflés out and place on a baking sheet lined with non-stick baking parchment. Dust with icing sugar and cook in a hot oven at 200°C (400°F) mark 6 for 15-20 minutes. Serve immediately on individual plates surrounded by the heather honey cream, decorated with the reserved blackberry juice.

REGIONAL HEATS

THE SOUTH WEST

DEREK JOHNS • TONY PURWIN • SUZANNE WYNN

WINNER

DEREK JOHNS' MENU

STARTER

Wood Pigeon Consommé, served in a Gourd

MAIN COURSE

Fake Fish in Filo, served with a Beurre Blanc Sauce

Mangetouts

French Beans

Baby Cauliflower

"I REALLY DID LIKE THE MAIN COURSE. I THOUGHT THE FISH WAS
A DELIGHT TO EAT" KEN RUSSELL

DESSERT

Poached Pears with a Vanilla Crème Anglaise
and Honey Sauce feathered with Chocolate

"I LOVED THE PUDDING. I THOUGHT THE PEAR WAS GREAT" LOYD

Derek Johns comes from Devizes in Wiltshire. Derek and his family are enthusiastic gardeners; he's recently completed a Revivalist Gravel Garden in the grounds of his impressive Queen Anne House. As a fine art dealer with a gallery in St James', Derek travels the world uncovering and restoring period paintings. Somehow he also manages to find time for his latest leisure pursuit – flying.

WOOD PIGEON CONSOMMÉ, SERVED IN A GOURD

1 wood pigeon, about 225 g (8 oz)
4 small gourds or squash

Consommé:
¼ chicken carcass (including wings, neck
  and legs, but not the breast, heart or liver)
125 g (4 oz) shin of beef, trimmed of fat
1 large carrot, finely chopped
1 leek, finely chopped
2 celery sticks, finely chopped
1.25 ml (¼ tsp) salt
freshly ground black pepper

Caramel:
25 g (1 oz) sugar

Vegetables:
2 white cabbage leaves
1 small courgette

To Garnish:
assorted salad leaves
snipped chives

Cut the breasts off the wood pigeon, remove the skin and set aside.

To make the consommé, break the wood pigeon and chicken carcasses into pieces and place in a large pan. Chop the beef and add to the pan together with the remaining consommé ingredients and about 1.75 litres (3 pints) cold water. Bring slowly to the boil, cover and simmer for 3 hours, skimming occasionally. Allow to cool and chill until the fat solidifies on the surface; remove the fat. Strain through a muslin-lined sieve to obtain a clear broth.

To prepare the gourds, cut a slice from the base of each one so that it will stand flat. Cut off the tops and reserve for the lids. Carefully scoop out the seeds and flesh, leaving a 2 cm (¾ inch) outer shell. Rinse the insides with hot water, drain and set aside.

Pour the consommé into a pan and bring to the boil. Cut the wood pigeon breasts into thin strips and add to the consommé. Simmer gently for 10 minutes.

Meanwhile prepare the caramel. Put the sugar in a small heavy-based pan and heat gently until dissolved, then cook for 5 minutes without stirring, until caramelised to a dark golden brown colour. Very carefully add 120 ml (4 fl oz) boiling water (the mixture will splutter) and bring to the boil, stirring, to melt the caramel. Add the caramel to the consommé to impart colour.

To prepare the vegetables, fold the cabbage leaves and cut the courgette into thin strips retaining the skin. Using a corrugated cutter, cut small decorative shapes from these vegetables. Add to the consommé and simmer for 2 minutes. Check the seasoning.

Just before serving, fill the gourds with boiling water and leave to stand for 1 minute to warm through. Arrange the salad leaves on individual serving plates. Drain the gourds and place one on each plate. Fill with the hot consommé, making sure each serving has a portion of meat strips and vegetable slivers. Sprinkle with snipped chives and replace the gourd lids. Serve at once.

FAKE FISH IN FILO, SERVED WITH A BEURRE BLANC SAUCE

4 lemon sole fillets, each about 75 g (3 oz), skinned
225 g (8 oz) salmon tail fillet, skinned
8 sheets of filo pastry
125 g (4 oz) butter, melted
salt and freshly ground black pepper
juice of ½ lime, to taste
16 coriander leaves
12 small sorrel or spinach leaves
4 currants

Beurre Blanc Sauce:
4 shallots, very finely diced
120 ml (4 fl oz) dry white wine
15 ml (1 tbsp) white wine vinegar
225 g (8 oz) butter, chilled and cut into small pieces

Cut the sole fillets lengthways into 8 strips, cut the salmon fillet lengthways into 4 strips.

Make the 4 fish parcels one at a time. Place a sheet of filo pastry lengthways towards you on the work surface and brush with melted butter. Put a strip of sole along the top of the filo sheet and season with salt and pepper. Sprinkle with a little lime juice and add 2 coriander leaves. Add a sorrel leaf (trimmed to the same size as the sole). Lay a strip of salmon on top. Season, sprinkle with lime juice and add 2 coriander leaves and a trimmed sorrel leaf. Cover with another layer of sole, sprinkle with lime juice and top with a sorrel layer.

From the top, fold the pastry down over the fish and continue folding, brushing with butter on each turn, to form a roll. Place another sheet of filo pastry on the work surface and brush with butter. Lay the fish roll along the top edge and roll up, brushing with butter with each turn, as before. The art is to transform this roll into a fish shape.

To do this, tuck in the pastry at one end to form the head end and pinch the filo towards the other end for the tail. Make cuts at the tail end to form tail fins. Using a sharp knife, carefully score through the outer sheet of filo only to outline the backbone, gills and scales. Repeat this process to make 4 'fake fish' in total. Insert a currant into each fish to resemble an eye.

Carefully transfer the 'fake fish' to a greased baking sheet. Bake in a preheated oven at 200°C (400°F) mark 6 for 15 minutes until crisp and golden.

To make the beurre blanc sauce, put the shallots, wine and vinegar in a small heavy-based pan and bring to the boil. Reduce by boiling until only about 30 ml (2 tbsp) liquid remains – just enough to moisten the shallots. Reduce the heat to as low as possible. Whisk in the butter, a piece at a time, making sure each one is thoroughly incorporated before adding the next, and whisking constantly, on and off the heat, to form a sauce which has the texture of mayonnaise.

To serve, transfer the 'fake fish' to warmed serving plates and flood the plates with the beurre blanc sauce. Arrange the accompanying vegetables on the plate in a decorative manner. Serve immediately.

POACHED PEARS, WITH A VANILLA CRÈME ANGLAISE AND HONEY SAUCE

75 g (3 oz) caster sugar
2 large Comice pears
lemon juice, for brushing
1 vanilla pod

Crème Anglaise:
6 egg yolks
75 g (3 oz) caster sugar
450 ml (¾ pint) milk
15 ml (1 tbsp) clear honey

To Finish:
125 g (4 oz) plain bitter chocolate, in pieces

Dissolve the sugar in 600 ml (1 pint) water in a saucepan over a low heat, then bring to a simmer. Meanwhile, peel, halve and core the pears and immediately brush with lemon juice to prevent discolouration. Add the pears to the sugar syrup with the vanilla pod and poach gently over a low heat for about 10 minutes; they should still be firm. Remove the vanilla pod and rinse. Leave the pears to cool in the syrup.

To make the crème anglaise, whisk the egg yolks and sugar together in a bowl for about 4 minutes until pale and creamy. Put the milk and rinsed vanilla pod in a pan and bring almost to the boil. Gradually add half of the milk to the egg and sugar mixture, whisking all the time. Stir into the remaining milk in the pan. Cook over a low heat for about 10 minutes, stirring continuously with a wooden spoon until it thickens enough to coat the back of the spoon. Strain through a fine sieve into a bowl. Stir in the honey. Cover the surface with a piece of damp greaseproof paper to prevent a skin forming and allow to cool.

Meanwhile put the chocolate and 100 ml (3½ fl oz) water in a heatproof bowl over a pan of simmering water until melted. Stir to form a smooth sauce.

To serve, drain the cooled pears and slice thinly, leaving the stalk end intact. Place one half flat-side down, in the centre of each plate and fan out slightly. Flood the plates with the crème anglaise. Pour a fine continuous circle of melted chocolate around each pear, then feather with a skewer or chopstick to create a decorative pattern. Serve at once.

REGIONAL HEATS
The South West

Derek Johns • Tony Purwin • Suzanne Wynn

Tony Purwin's Menu

STARTER

Batter Dumpling with Chives, served with a Red Pepper Coulis

"THIS STARTER IS VERY STRIKING. THE DUMPLINGS WERE A NICE IDEA"
DARINA ALLEN

MAIN COURSE

Fillet of Beef stuffed with Oysters, served with a
Claret and Oyster sauce
Caramelised Potatoes
Medallions of Green Vegetables
Carrot Julienne

DESSERT

Ricotta Hearts with Pistachios and Kirsch, served with
Raspberry and Mango Purées

"THE PISTACHIOS INSIDE WERE DELICIOUS" LOYD

Tony Purwin is an insurance broker from Dorchester in Dorset. The Purwin family are regular visitors to the seafront in nearby Weymouth, where Tony sometimes takes to the water to indulge his enthusiasm for sea fishing. In earlier days Tony was a lead guitarist in a pop group, and he still enjoys playing to the children.

BATTER DUMPLINGS WITH CHIVES, SERVED WITH A RED PEPPER COULIS

Dumplings:
150 g (5 oz) plain flour
1 egg, size 3
120 ml (4 fl oz) milk and water mixed
45 ml (3 tbsp) chopped chives
salt and freshly ground white pepper

Topping:
25 g (1 oz) butter, melted
50 g (2 oz) Gruyère cheese, grated
25 g (1 oz) fresh breadcrumbs

Red Pepper Coulis:
2 red peppers
1 small red chilli
120 ml (4 fl oz) white wine
1 large garlic clove, chopped
25 g (1 oz) fresh breadcrumbs
45 ml (3 tbsp) olive oil

To Garnish:
shredded lettuce

To make the dumplings, sift the flour into a bowl and make a well in the centre. Add the egg and half of the liquid and beat until smooth. Stir in the remaining liquid. Beat in the chives, then season with salt and pepper.

Bring a large pan of salted water to the boil. Drop spoonfuls of batter into the water, using a dampened teaspoon. Cook for 8-10 minutes, drain well and keep warm.

To make the pepper coulis, place the red peppers under a preheated hot grill and grill, turning frequently, until the skin is charred. Cover and leave until cool, then peel off the skins. Halve, remove the cores and seeds, then roughly chop the flesh. Blanch the chilli briefly in boiling water, then halve, seed and chop.

Reduce the wine by boiling to 60 ml (2 fl oz). Combine the pepper, chilli and garlic in a blender, and purée to a smooth paste. Blend in the bread-crumbs, a tablespoonful at a time, then blend in the olive oil a tablespoonful at a time. Finally repeat with the reduced white wine. Season with salt and pepper to taste. Heat through gently before serving.

Arrange the dumplings in a single layer in a greased gratin dish (brushed with some of the melted butter). Spoon the remaining butter over the top, season with salt and pepper, then sprinkle with the cheese and breadcrumbs. Place under a hot grill for 5 minutes, or until the topping is golden brown.

To serve, cover the base of each serving plate with red pepper coulis and arrange the dumplings in a circle on top. Place a ball of shredded lettuce in the centre to garnish.

FILLET OF BEEF STUFFED WITH OYSTERS, WITH A CLARET AND OYSTER SAUCE

575 g (1¼ lb) fillet of beef
salt and freshly ground black pepper
12 oysters
juice of 1 lemon, or to taste
30 ml (2 tbsp) olive oil

Claret and Oyster Sauce:

25 g (1 oz) butter
1 shallot, chopped
1 clove garlic, bruised
2 strips of finely pared lemon rind,
*   each 2.5 x 1 cm (1 x ½ inch)*
pinch of freshly grated nutmeg
pinch of cayenne pepper
50 g (2 oz) mushrooms, chopped
2 anchovy fillets, pounded
325 ml (11 fl oz) beef stock
375 ml (13 fl oz) claret
450 ml (¾ pint) double cream
lemon juice, to taste

To Garnish:

watercress sprigs

Trim the beef of all fat, then make a lengthways cut along the side of the beef, three quarters through. Open out and season with salt and pepper.

Open the oysters and reserve the beards and liquor. Lay about six of the oysters, overlapping along the open fillet to within 2 cm (¾ inch) of each end. (Reserve the other oysters for the sauce.) Sprinkle the oysters and fillet with lemon juice. Reshape meat, to enclose oysters and tie at 2.5 cm (1 inch) intervals with string. Cover and set aside.

To make the sauce, melt the butter in a pan. Add the shallot, garlic, lemon rind, nutmeg and cayenne. Cook over a low heat for 2-3 minutes until the onions are soft. Add the mushrooms and cook for 1 minute. Stir in the anchovies, oyster beards and liquor. Simmer for 2 minutes.

Add the reserved oysters and poach gently in the liquor for 1-2 minutes or until the edges begin to curl. Remove with a slotted spoon and set aside.

Add the beef stock and all but 45 ml (3 tbsp) claret to the pan and reduce by half, or until the liquid is of a syrupy consistency. Add the cream and reduce again until the sauce is thick enough to coat the back of a spoon. You should have about 400 ml (14 fl oz). Strain the sauce through a fine sieve into a clean bowl and keep warm over a steamer.

Purée the reserved oysters in a blender or food processor with the remaining 45 ml (3 tbsp) claret. Stir into the sauce. Add lemon juice, salt and pepper to taste.

To cook the beef, heat the oil in a heavy-based frying pan. Season the fillet with salt and pepper, then add to the pan and sear over a high heat on all sides. Transfer to a rack over a roasting tin, containing 150 ml (¼ pint) warm water.

Roast in a preheated oven at 220°C (425°F) mark 7 for 15-20 minutes. Cover and leave to stand in a warm place for 20 minutes, before carving into slices.

To serve, spoon a little of the sauce on to each plate and arrange the beef slices on top. Garnish with watercress.

CARAMELISED POTATOES

450 g (1 lb) small new potatoes
30 ml (2 tbsp) oil
30 ml (2 tbsp) granulated sugar

Boil the potatoes in their skins in salted water for about 10 minutes until just tender. Set aside to cool, then peel.

Heat the oil in a frying pan, sprinkle the sugar over the base of the pan and cook until lightly browned. Add the potatoes and fry, stirring, for about 5 minutes until golden brown. Drain on kitchen paper and serve immediately.

Medallions of Green Vegetables

4 large cabbage leaves
4 large spinach leaves
4 large lettuce leaves
salt and freshly ground black pepper

Bring a large pan of salted water to the boil. Blanch the cabbage leaves, two at a time, for 3 minutes. Remove with a slotted spoon and refresh in cold water, then dry on kitchen paper.

Blanch the spinach leaves in the same way, for 1 minute. Drain, refresh in cold water and dry on kitchen paper.

Remove any thick stems from the cabbage and spinach leaves. Lay the cabbage leaves out flat on a board.

Place a spinach leaf and a lettuce leaf on top of each cabbage leaf, then season with salt and pepper. Roll up the leaves from the stem end and tie with string.

Place the leaf rolls in a steamer over the pan of boiling water and steam for 3-4 minutes until cooked, but retaining some bite. Remove the string and cut four 2 cm (¾ inch) slices from each roll. Serve immediately, cut side up.

Ricotta Hearts with Pistachios and Kirsch, served with Raspberry and Mango Purées

225 g (8 oz) ricotta cheese
60 ml (4 tbsp) icing sugar, sifted
1.25 ml (¼ tsp) vanilla extract
30 ml (2 tbsp) pistachio nuts, chopped
30 ml (2 tbsp) kirsch
150 ml (¼ pint) double cream
450 g (1 lb) raspberries, hulled
1 large ripe mango
4 mint sprigs, to decorate

Line 4 heart-shaped moulds with dampened squares of muslin, which are large enough to overhang the sides.

Pass the ricotta cheese through a sieve into a bowl and beat until light and fluffy, then beat in 30 ml (2 tbsp) icing sugar and the vanilla extract. Fold in the pistachio nuts and kirsch, until evenly blended. Whip the double cream until thick, then fold into the cheese mixture.

Fill the lined moulds with the cheese mixture, piling it into a slight dome in the centre. Fold the muslin over the top to enclose and chill for at least 1 hour.

Set aside 2 large raspberries for decoration. Using the back of a ladle, press the remaining raspberries through a sieve into a bowl to remove the seeds. Stir in 15 ml (1 tbsp) icing sugar.

Peel, halve and stone the mango, then press the flesh through a sieve into a bowl. Add the remaining 15 ml (1 tbsp) icing sugar and stir well.

To serve, unmould each cheese dessert on to a flat dessert plate and carefully remove the muslin. Pour a circle of raspberry purée around each cheese heart, followed by a circle of mango purée. Using the tip of a knife, feather the fruit purées together decoratively. Top each cheese heart with a halved raspberry and a mint sprig. Serve immediately.

REGIONAL HEATS

The South West

Derek Johns • Tony Purwin • Suzanne Wynn

Suzanne Wynn's Menu

Starter

Leek and Mussel Soup

"The soup had a nice cool taste and colour" Loyd

Main Course

Roast Breast of Duck, served with a Confit of Duck
Potato and Celeriac Rösti
Quince Tartlets
Braised Red Cabbage

Dessert

Banana Baked en Papilotte with Mango and Passion Fruit
Vanilla Ice Cream

"It was a totally new experience to have all these fruits combined in their juices" Ken Russell

---

Suzanne Wynn from Bristol is a senior training officer with a national Building Society. To get away from it all at weekends, Suzanne goes horse riding in nearby Blagdon. Clay pigeon shooting is Suzanne's other sport, which she enjoys with her husband, Ian.

LEEK AND MUSSEL SOUP

1.4 kg (3 lb) mussels
6 leeks
25 g (1 oz) butter
15 ml (1 tbsp) diced carrot
15 ml (1 tbsp) diced onion
15 ml (1 tbsp) diced celery
½ small potato, peeled and chopped
600 ml (1 pint) fish stock
1 shallot, chopped
1 thyme sprig
1 parsley sprig
¼ bay leaf
150 ml (¼ pint) white wine
salt and freshly ground black pepper

To Garnish:
chopped chives

Scrub the mussels thoroughly in cold water and remove their beards.

Chop 5 leeks. Heat the butter in a pan, add the chopped leeks, carrot, onion and celery and sweat them gently for 5 minutes. Add the potato and fish stock and cook, uncovered, for about 25 minutes until the leeks are completely soft. Purée in a blender or food processor and pass the mixture through a sieve.

Put the shallot, herbs, mussels and white wine in a large saucepan. Cover tightly and cook over a high heat for 5 minutes, shaking the pan from time to time. Remove from the heat and discard any mussels that have not opened. Strain the liquor through a muslin-lined sieve to remove any grit. Remove the mussels from their shells. Add the strained liquor and mussels to the leek purée. Reheat, then season with salt and pepper to taste.

Shred the remaining leek and steam briefly for 2-3 minutes until tender. Divide the leek between warmed soup bowls, then pour in the soup. Garnish with chopped chives to serve.

CONFIT OF DUCK

This preserved confit needs to be prepared a week in advance. It is served as an accompaniment to the main course.

4 whole duck legs
20 g (¾ oz) coarse sea salt
2 thyme sprigs
2 bay leaves
2.5 ml (½ tsp) freshly ground black pepper
2.5 ml (½ tsp) freshly grated nutmeg
700 g (1½ lb) goose or duck fat
(approximately)

Rub each duck leg with salt and lay in a dish. Sprinkle with the remaining salt, herbs, pepper and nutmeg. Cover and leave in the refrigerator overnight.

The next day, wipe the excess salt from the duck and lay skin-side down in a flameproof casserole. Cook over a low heat for 15-20 minutes until the fat runs and the duck is lightly browned. Add sufficient fat to cover the duck and cook in a preheated oven at 150°C (300°F) mark 2 for 2 hours until the duck is very tender and has rendered all of its fat.

Pour a layer of the fat into the base of a terrine or dish which will hold the duck legs snugly. Leave until set then pack in the duck and pour over enough fat to cover completely. Cover and leave in the refrigerator for at least 1 week to allow the flavour to develop.

To serve, leave the confit in a warm place until the fat starts to run. Heat a little of the fat in a heavy-based frying pan and fry the duck legs over a very high heat until the skin is crisp and brown. Serve immediately.

ROAST BREAST OF DUCK

For this recipe try to obtain Gressingham, Lunesdale or Challen ducks. I serve the duck with a preserved confit (see page 107) which needs to be prepared a week in advance to allow the flavours to develop. Either buy the ducks a week in advance and freeze the duck breasts and carcasses until required, or make your confit from other duck legs.

2 ducks, each about 2 kg (4½ lb)
1 onion
1 carrot
1 celery stick
2-3 parsley sprigs
1 thyme sprig
1 bay leaf
4 black peppercorns
salt and freshly ground black pepper
150 ml (¼ pint) red wine

Remove the breasts and whole legs from the ducks. Use the legs to make a confit (see page 107). Reserve the carcasses.

Roughly chop the vegetables and place in a large saucepan with the duck carcasses, herbs, peppercorns and salt. Add cold water to cover, bring to the boil and skim. Simmer gently for about 2 hours. Strain the stock through a fine sieve, then using a gravy separator, carefully pour off 600 ml (1 pint) stock leaving the fat behind. Alternatively pour off the fat from the surface, then measure the quantity of stock needed.

Pour the stock into a clean pan and boil vigorously until reduced by about one third. Add the red wine and continue to boil until the sauce is reduced and thickened. Taste and adjust the seasoning.

To cook the duck, heat a heavy-based frying pan, then place the duck breasts skin-side down in the pan. Cook over a medium heat for about 1 minute until some of the fat has been rendered and the skin is slightly browned. Turn the breasts over and cook briefly to seal them.

Transfer the duck breasts to a rack over a roasting tin and place in a preheated oven at 200°C (400°F) mark 6 for 8 minutes. Cover with foil and leave to rest for 15-20 minutes. (The breasts can be briefly flashed under a hot grill to brown the skin and reheat before carving if necessary.)

To serve, carve the duck breasts and arrange on warmed serving plates. Spoon on a small amount of the sauce and serve with the confit of duck, and accompaniments.

Note: To save time, prepare the stock in a pressure cooker. Cook at high pressure for about 40 minutes.

POTATO AND CELERIAC RÖSTI

4 small potatoes, preferably King Edwards
125 g (4 oz) celeriac
salt and freshly ground black pepper
30 ml (2 tbsp) duck fat or butter

Peel and finely grate the potatoes and celeriac. Mix together and season well with salt and pepper. Divide into 4 portions. Shape each portion into an oval in a piece of kitchen paper to remove excess moisture.

Heat the duck fat in a frying pan, then add the potato and celeriac ovals, drawing in any stray pieces to keep their shape. Fry over a moderate heat for about 5 minutes until crisp and golden brown underneath, then turn over and fry the other side until cooked. Drain on kitchen paper. Serve at once.

BRAISED RED CABBAGE

350 g (12 oz) red cabbage
½ cooking apple
20 g (¾ oz) butter
1 small onion, finely chopped
30 ml (2 tbsp) brown sugar
45 ml (3 tbsp) red wine vinegar
45 ml (3 tbsp) red wine
1.25 ml (¼ tsp) ground cinnamon
1.25 ml (¼ tsp) freshly grated nutmeg
pinch of ground cloves
salt and freshly ground black pepper

Shred the red cabbage. Peel, core and chop the apple. Heat the butter in a pan, add the cabbage, apple and onion and cook, stirring for 2-3 minutes. Add the remaining ingredients, then transfer the mixture to a casserole dish. Cook in a preheated oven at 160°C (325°F) mark 3 for about 2 hours until tender, stirring once or twice during cooking.

QUINCE TARTLETS

1-2 quinces, depending on size
25 g (1 oz) sugar
15 ml (1 tbsp) quince jelly (approximately)

Pastry:
125 g (4 oz) plain flour
pinch of salt
25 g (1 oz) butter
25 g (1 oz) white vegetable fat

Roughly chop the quinces and place them in an ovenproof dish with the sugar. Cover and cook in a preheated oven at 160°C (325°F) mark 3 for about 1 hour until very tender.

Meanwhile make the pastry for the tartlet cases. Sift the flour and salt into a bowl, then rub in the butter and white fat until the mixture resembles fine breadcrumbs. Using a round-bladed knife, stir in about 15 ml (1 tbsp) cold water to bind the dough together. Cover and leave to rest in a cool place for 30 minutes.

Roll out the pastry thinly on a lightly floured surface and use to line 4 tartlet tins, 5 cm (2 inches) in diameter. Prick the bases with a fork. Line with grease-proof paper and baking beans and bake blind in a preheated oven at 200°C (400°F) mark 6 for 10 minutes. Remove the paper and beans and return to the oven for 10-15 minutes or until cooked through.

Purée the quinces in a food processor then press through a sieve into a pan. Add quince jelly to sweeten, heating gently to help melt the jelly; the purée should still be slightly sharp. Fill the baked tartlet cases with the quince purée to serve.

BANANAS BAKED EN PAPILOTTE WITH MANGO AND PASSION FRUIT

For these papilottes you will need 4 pieces of foil, about 60 cm (2 feet) long – cut from a standard width roll of foil.

1 ripe mango
8 passion fruit
juice of ½ orange
75 g (3 oz) caster sugar
4 bananas
juice of ¼ lemon
1 vanilla pod

Peel the mango and cut into fairly large chunks, discarding the stone. Put a quarter of the mango pieces in a food processor. Halve the passion fruit and scoop out the pulp and seeds into the processor. Add the orange juice and sugar. Process until the mango is puréed, then pass through a sieve to remove the passion fruit seeds.

Cut 4 pieces of foil, about 60 x 30 cm (24 x 12 inches). Fold each one in half, to make 30 cm (12 inch) squares. Halve the bananas lengthwise and lay one piece on the lower half of each foil square. Sprinkle with a little lemon juice. Divide the mango chunks between the parcels.

Cut the vanilla pod into 4 pieces, then split open. Using a knife, scrape out the vanilla seeds and place on the banana. Include a piece of vanilla pod in each parcel. Spoon the mango and passion fruit purée over the banana and fold the top half of the foil over.

Starting at the top left corner begin neatly folding in the foil to seal the package. Continue until only the top right corner is left open, then blow into the package to inflate it before sealing.

Bake in a preheated oven at 190°C (375°F) mark 5 for 10 minutes. Let your guests slit open the parcels to reveal the contents! Serve with vanilla ice cream.

VANILLA ICE CREAM

300 ml (½ pint) milk
1 vanilla pod
125 g (4 oz) sugar
6 egg yolks
200 ml (7 fl oz) double cream

Pour the milk into a saucepan. Split the vanilla pod and scrape out the seeds into the milk; add the pod as well. Heat the milk and vanilla pod until simmering, then remove from the heat and leave to infuse for 30 minutes. Strain through a fine sieve.

Dissolve the sugar in 200 ml (7 fl oz) water in a heavy-based pan over a low heat. Bring to the boil and boil steadily to a fairly thick syrup.

Whisk the egg yolks in a large bowl until pale and creamy. Slowly pour in the hot sugar syrup in a steady stream, whisking all the time. Whisk in the milk, then leave the mixture until cool.

Add the cream, then turn into an ice-cream maker and freeze until firm.

Alternatively if you do not have an ice-cream maker, whip the cream lightly before folding in. Turn into a freezer-proof container, cover and place in the freezer until the mixture is beginning to freeze around the edges. Turn out into a bowl and whisk to break down the ice crystals, then return to the freezer until almost firm. Turn out into a bowl and beat the mixture again, before returning to the freezer until firm. Allow to soften at room temperature for about 15 minutes before serving.

REGIONAL HEATS
THE HOME COUNTIES
TONY DAVIS • JANET DIMMER • ANNE HEATON

WINNER

TONY DAVIS' MENU

STARTER

Harlequin Omelette

"REALLY NICE COMBINATION OF FLAVOURS" JENNI MURRAY

MAIN COURSE

Breast of Chicken with Comté Cheese Sauce
Fresh Spinach Tagliatelle

"THIS DISH INVITES REAL EATING" GARY RHODES

DESSERT

Normandy Pear Tart with Almond Cream

"THE PEARS REALLY TASTE LIKE PEARS IN THIS DISH" GARY RHODES

Tony Davis from Harrow in Middlesex, is a computer sales training consultant. Tony studied at the Royal Academy of Music and now plays that notoriously difficult instrument, the French horn, with a group of friends calling themselves 'Classics Revisited'. He is an enthusiastic photographer, and has cunningly converted a garden shed to a darkroom for his colour processing.

HARLEQUIN OMELETTE

500 g (1 lb 2 oz) young spinach leaves
400 g (14 oz) tomatoes
120 ml (8 tbsp) olive oil
pinch of finely chopped thyme
salt and freshly ground black pepper
2 cloves garlic, peeled
9 eggs
120 ml (8 tbsp) whipping cream
pinch of freshly grated nutmeg
75 g (3 oz) Gruyère cheese, finely grated

To Serve:
salad leaves
black olives
a little extra-virgin olive oil

Clean the spinach thoroughly. Skin, deseed and coarsely chop the tomatoes. Heat 30 ml (2 tbsp) olive oil in a saucepan. Add the chopped tomatoes wiih a little thyme and a pinch of salt. Cook until all moisture has evaporated.

Meanwhile, heat 45 ml (3 tbsp) olive oil in another saucepan. Add the spinach, garlic and a pinch of salt. Stir until the moisture has completely evaporated. When the tomatoes and spinach are cooked, put them on separate plates. Discard the garlic from the spinach. Allow to cool.

Break 3 eggs into each of 3 bowls. To the first bowl add the spinach, 45 ml (3 tbsp) cream, freshly grated nutmeg, salt and pepper. Whisk together thoroughly.

To the second bowl, add the tomatoes, 30 ml (2 tbsp) cream, salt and pepper; whisk together.

To the third bowl, add the grated Gruyère, 45 ml (3 tbsp) cream and salt and pepper; whisk together.

Liberally oil a 30 x 10 cm (10 x 4 inch) terrine dish. Pour in the tomato mixture, cover and steam in a steamer over boiling water for 15 minutes. Then, carefully, pour in the cheese mixture and

steam for a further 15 minutes. Finally, pour in the spinach mixture and cook for 20 minutes or until the top is firm and a skewer inserted into the middle of the 'omelette' comes out cleanly.

Allow to rest for 10-15 minutes before turning out. Cut into slices and serve warm or cold on a bed of salad leaves, garnished with a few black olives. Trickle a little olive oil over each slice.

BREAST OF CHICKEN WITH COMTÉ CHEESE SAUCE

4 boneless chicken breasts, skinned
salt and freshly ground black pepper
flour for coating
60 g (2½ oz) butter
350 ml (12 fl oz) dry white wine
300 ml (½ pint) chicken stock
pinch of freshly grated nutmeg
pinch of cayenne pepper

Comté Cheese Sauce:
45 g (1¼ oz) butter
25 g (1 oz) plain flour
2 egg yolks
150 ml (¼ pint) crème fraîche
30 g (1 oz) Comté cheese, finely grated

To Finish:
60 g (2-2½ oz) Comté cheese, grated
blanched red pepper diamonds

Cut the chicken breasts into bite-sized pieces. Season with salt and pepper and coat evenly with flour, shaking off any excess. Heat the butter in a wide, shallow pan and brown the chicken pieces on all sides over a medium heat. Stir in the white wine; bring to the boil, then add the chicken stock with the nutmeg and cayenne. Bring to a simmer and gently poach the chicken pieces for a few minutes until tender. Remove the chicken with a slotted spoon and trans-

Fillet of Sea Bass with Gooseberry and Nutmeg Sauce
KERRY CHURCH'S MAIN COURSE (SEMI-FINAL)

Tagliatelle with Globe Artichoke and Wild Mushrooms
DEREK JOHNS' STARTER (FINAL)

fer to a greased 1.5 litre (2½ pint) baking dish. Skim off the fat from the cooking liquid. Strain the liquid and reserve.

To make the sauce, melt the butter in a saucepan and stir in the flour. Let it bubble for 1 minute, then gradually whisk in the strained cooking liquid. Simmer, stirring occasionally, for 5-10 minutes until thickened to a coating consistency. Check the seasoning.

In a bowl, beat the egg yolks with the crème fraîche. Whisk a little of the sauce into the yolk mixture, then whisk this mixture into the remaining sauce. Heat gently, without boiling, until slightly thickened. Remove from the heat and add the Comté cheese, stirring until melted. Check the seasoning.

Pour the sauce over the chicken. Sprinkle with grated cheese and bake in a preheated oven at 220°C (425°F) mark 7 for 5 minutes until golden brown.

Arrange on warmed plates, and garnish with red pepper diamonds. Serve immediately with spinach tagliatelle.

Note: For the red pepper garnish, blanch diamonds of seeded red pepper in boiling water for 1 minute, then refresh in cold water and drain.

FRESH SPINACH TAGLIATELLE

This delicious homemade pasta is simple to make, using a pasta machine. It is only really worth attempting if you have a pasta machine. Otherwise buy freshly made pasta from a good Italian delicatessen.

225 g (8 oz) young spinach
350 g (12 oz) pasta flour "type 00"
2.5 ml (½ tsp) salt
2 eggs, size 2

To Serve:
15 ml (1 tbsp) olive oil or melted butter

Clean the spinach thoroughly, discarding the stems. Place in a pan with only the water clinging to the leaves after washing. Cover and cook for 8-10 minutes, shaking the pan occasionally. Drain thoroughly in a sieve, pressing out as much liquid as possible; reserve the liquid. Put the spinach in a food processor or blender with 15 ml (1 tbsp) of the reserved juice and work to a purée. Turn into a bowl and leave to cool.

To make the pasta dough, sift the flour and salt into a bowl and make a well in the centre. Add the eggs and puréed spinach. Mix together to form a dough. Knead on a lightly floured surface until the dough is smooth; this will take about 10 minutes.

Place the dough on a plate, cover with a bowl and leave to rest at room temperature for 1 hour, or leave overnight on the bottom shelf of the refrigerator.

Cut off a portion of the dough and feed it through your pasta machine to the required thickness, then pass through the tagliatelle cutter. Hang on a pasta dryer (or a suspended piece of wooden dowel) to dry for about 15 minutes before cooking.

Cook the tagliatelle in a large pan of boiling salted water for a few minutes until *al dente* (tender but firm to the bite). Drain thoroughly and toss the pasta with a little olive oil or butter. Serve immediately.

NORMANDY PEAR TART WITH ALMOND CREAM

2 ripe firm pears

Pastry:
200 g (7 oz) plain flour
1.25 ml (¼ tsp) salt
100 g (3½ oz) butter
1 egg yolk

Almond Cream:
100 g (3½ oz) butter
100 g (3½ oz) sugar
1 egg, beaten
1 egg yolk
10 ml (2 tsp) kirsch
100 g (3½ oz) ground almonds
15 g (½ oz) plain flour

To Finish:
caster sugar, for sprinkling
75 ml (5 tbsp) apricot glaze (see note)

First make the pastry. Sift the flour and salt into a bowl and rub in the butter until the mixture resembles fine breadcrumbs. Using a round-bladed knife, mix in the egg yolk with 35-45 ml (2½-3 tbsp) cold water to bind the pastry. Wrap in cling film or foil and chill in the refrigerator for 30 minutes.

Roll out the pastry and use to line four 10 cm (4 inch) individual fluted flan tins. Chill for 10 minutes. Place a baking sheet in the oven set at 200°C (400°F) mark 6 to preheat.

To make the almond cream, cream the butter in a mixing bowl until soft. Add the sugar gradually, beating constantly, until light and soft. Beat in the egg and egg yolk, followed by the kirsch. Fold in the ground almonds and flour. Pour two thirds of the mixture into the 4 flan cases, dividing it equally and spreading evenly.

Peel the pears, halve and remove the core and stems. Place each pear, cut side down, on a board and cut into fine slices, keeping the stem ends intact. Halve each piece and press lightly to fan out, maintaining the pear shape. Arrange one complete pear half in each flan tin. Spoon the remaining almond cream around each half pear.

Place the flan tins on the preheated baking sheet and bake at 200°C (400°F) mark 6 for 10-15 minutes until the pastry begins to brown lightly. Lower the oven temperature to 175°C (335°F) mark 3½ and bake for a further 10 minutes until the pears are tender and the almond cream is set.

Sprinkle the pears liberally with sugar and bake for a further 20 minutes until the sugar caramelises slightly. Transfer the flans to a wire rack to cool. Before serving, brush with apricot glaze. Serve at room temperature.

Note: To make an apricot glaze, heat 75 ml (5 tbsp) apricot jam with 15 ml (1 tbsp) water in a small pan until melted. Bring to the boil, then sieve before use.

REGIONAL HEATS

THE HOME COUNTIES

TONY DAVIS • JANET DIMMER • ANNE HEATON

JANET DIMMER'S MENU

STARTER

Onion Leaves stuffed with Date Sauce, served with
Dill-stuffed Sugar Snap Peas

"PUTTING ONIONS AND DATES TOGETHER WAS A VERY INTERESTING IDEA"
JENNI MURRAY

MAIN COURSE

Pecan and Chestnut Casserole in Red Wine
Wild Rice with Red Pepper Sauce
Stir-fried Mangetouts with Garlic

"THIS REALLY HAD GOOD FLAVOURS AND TEXTURES" JENNI MURRAY

DESSERT

Raspberry Roulade with Chilled Raspberry Sauce

Janet Dimmer comes from the delightful village of
Shamley Green in Surrey. For two years Janet lived in
Bermuda where she was the demon bowler of the local cricket
team. She still plays cricket and keeps up her fitness by
running. Janet and her husband, Simon, are both accountants
with a home-based business.

Onion Leaves stuffed with Date Sauce, served with Dill-stuffed Sugar Snap Peas

4 onions
200 ml (⅓ pint) dry white wine (approximately)

Date Sauce:
50 g (2 oz) stoned dates
30 ml (2 tbsp) lemon juice
2.5 ml (½ tsp) ground cumin
2.5 ml (½ tsp) chilli powder

Dill-stuffed Sugar Snaps:
8 sugar snap peas
15 ml (1 tbsp) fromage frais
30 ml (2 tbsp) crème fraîche
10 ml (2 tsp) lime juice
10 ml (2 tsp) chopped dill

To Garnish:
dill sprigs

First make the onion leaves. After peeling the onions, make a single cut in each one from the top to the base, cutting right into the core of the onion. Add to a pan of boiling water and simmer for 10 minutes, drain and refresh in cold water, then drain well. Cut off the root ends with a sharp knife and discard, then separate the onions into leaves.

To make the date sauce, combine all the ingredients in a saucepan with 90 ml (3 fl oz) water and bring to the boil. Lower the heat, cover and simmer for 10 minutes. Transfer to a blender or food processor and work until smooth.

Put a tablespoonful of date sauce into each onion leaf, roll up and place in a shallow casserole. Add just sufficient wine to half cover the onion leaves. Cover and cook in a preheated oven at 220°C (425°F) mark 7 for 40 minutes basting and turning halfway through cooking. Uncover the dish 10 minutes before the end of the cooking time.

Blanch the sugar snap peas in boiling water for 2 minutes, then drain and refresh in cold water; drain well. In a bowl, mix together the fromage frais, crème fraîche, lime juice and dill. Split the peas along one side and carefully fill with the stuffing.

To serve, arrange the onion leaves on individual plates in the shape of a flower head, using the stuffed peas as leaves and dill as the stalks.

PECAN AND CHESTNUT CASSEROLE IN RED WINE

125 g (4 oz) dried chestnuts
125 g (4 oz) carrots
125 g (4 oz) baby onions
45 ml (3 tbsp) olive oil
30 ml (2 tbsp) chopped mixed herbs (sage, rosemary and thyme)
300 ml (½ pint) red wine
50 g (2 oz) buckwheat
175 g (6 oz) button mushroms
50 g (2 oz) gram flour
15 ml (1 tbsp) soy sauce
175 g (6 oz) Brussel sprouts
125 g (4 oz) pecan nuts

To Garnish:
rosemary and thyme sprigs

Put the dried chestnuts in a saucepan with 1.2 litres (2 pints) of water and bring to the boil. Cover and simmer for 25-30 minutes. Drain, reserving the liquid.

Meanwhile cut the carrots into pieces, similar in size to the onions. Heat 30 ml (2 tbsp) oil in a flameproof casserole, add the whole baby onions and fry, stirring for about 3 minutes. Add the carrots and fry the onions and carrots together over a low heat for a few minutes, turning them in the oil.

Add the chestnuts and reserved liquid together with the herbs and a third of the red wine. Cover and cook in a preheated oven at 190°C (375°F) mark 5 for 25 minutes.

Heat 15 ml (1 tbsp) olive oil in a frying pan and stir-fry the buckwheat for 3 minutes. Add the mushrooms and fry, stirring, for a further 2 minutes.

Bring the remaining red wine to the boil in a small pan and sprinkle in the gram flour. Simmer, stirring, for 3-5 minutes until the wine begins to thicken, then add the soy sauce.

Add the thickened red wine to the casserole with the buckwheat, mushrooms, Brussel sprouts and pecan nuts. Return to the oven for a further 20 minutes. Sprinkle with pepper and garnish with rosemary and thyme. Serve with the accompaniments.

WILD RICE WITH RED PEPPER SAUCE

125 g (4 oz) wild rice
125 g (4 oz) brown basmati rice
2 red peppers
freshly ground black pepper

Put the wild rice and brown basmati rice together in a saucepan with 525 ml (18 fl oz) water. Bring to the boil, lower the heat, cover and simmer for 35 minutes without removing the lid or stirring, until the rice is tender and the water is completely absorbed.

Meanwhile, quarter the red peppers, discarding the core and seeds. Place the pepper quarters, skin-side up, under a very hot grill (or in a hot oven) until blackened and blistered. Cover with a plate or tea-towel until cool enough to handle, then peel away the skin. Purée the pepper flesh with a little water in a blender or food processor until smooth. Add pepper to taste.

Lightly brush 4 warmed dariole moulds with olive oil. Spoon the rice mixture into the oiled moulds, pressing down gently, then immediately turn out onto warmed plates. Pour the red pepper sauce around the rice and spoon a small amount over the top of the rice. Serve at once.

STIR-FRIED MANGETOUTS WITH GARLIC

Mangetouts have such a lovely taste
and texture that they need no additional
flavouring.

225 g (8 oz) mangetouts
15 ml (1 tbsp) olive oil
2 cloves garlic, finely chopped

Top and tail the mangetouts. Heat the olive oil in a wok or deep frying pan and stir-fry the garlic for 2 minutes. Add the mangetouts together with 30 ml (2 tbsp) water and stir-fry for 2 minutes. Serve immediately.

RASPBERRY ROULADE WITH CHILLED RASPBERRY SAUCE

Roulade:
3 eggs
75 g (3 oz) brown sugar
75 g (3 oz) brown self-raising flour
75 g (3 oz) ground almonds

Sauce, Filling and Topping:
225 g (8 oz) raspberries
50 g (2 oz) brown sugar
225 g (8 oz) ricotta cheese
30 ml (2 tbsp) yogurt
flaked almonds, to decorate
icing sugar, for dusting

Line a 30 x 20 cm (12 x 8 inch) Swiss roll tin with non-stick baking parchment.

To make the roulade, whisk the eggs and sugar together in a large bowl, using an electric whisk, for 8 minutes. Sift the flour and ground almonds together and lightly fold into the whisked mixture, with 15 ml (1 tbsp) hot water. Pour the mixture into the prepared tin and bake in a preheated oven at 200°C (400°F) mark 6 for 8-10 minutes until springy to the touch.

Meanwhile make the raspberry sauce. Put 125 g (4 oz) of the raspberries in a saucepan with the sugar over a low heat, mashing the fruit slightly as the sugar dissolves. Leave to simmer gently for 20 minutes.

Cover a damp tea-towel with a sheet of non-stick baking parchment and sprinkle with brown sugar. When the roulade is cooked, turn it out on to the paper and carefully peel off the lining paper. Trim off the crusty edges. Roll up the sponge gently, from a short side, enclosing the paper and using the tea-towel to help you roll. Place on a wire rack to cool.

Pass the raspberry sauce through a nylon sieve to remove the seeds, allow to cool, then chill.

Beat the ricotta cheese with the yogurt in a bowl until smooth. Carefully unroll the roulade and remove the paper; do not worry if it cracks. Set aside about a quarter of the ricotta mixture for decoration; spread the rest over the roulade to within 2.5 cm (1 inch) of the edges. (Do not spread it right to the edges otherwise it will ooze out later.) Halve the remaining raspberries; set aside some for decoration. Sprinkle the rest over the ricotta filling.

Carefully roll up the roulade enclosing the filling and place on a serving dish. Pipe the remaining ricotta mixture along the top and decorate with flaked almonds and raspberries. Sprinkle with icing sugar.

To serve, cut the roulade into slices and arrange on individual plates on a pool of raspberry sauce.

Regional Heats
The Home Counties
Tony Davis • Janet Dimmer • Anne Heaton

Anne Heaton's Menu

Starter
Scallops on a Julienne of Vegetables with a Mousseline Sauce

Main Course
Best End of Lamb in a Port and Rosemary Demi-glace Sauce
Carrot Ribbons
Spinach Darioles
Celeriac Purée in Filo Cases
Sauté Potatoes
"Excellent flavouring" Loyd

Dessert
Provençal Lavender Honey and Ginger Ice Cream with
Chocolate Sauce and Raspberry Coulis, served in
Brandy Snap Baskets
"The ice cream was out of this world" Jenni Murray

A nne Heaton lives in Iver in Buckinghamshire. Anne is a director of a marketing and management consultancy with involvement in exhibitions throughout Europe. She is also an experienced pilot. Anne's latest hobby is reupholstering, and she is currently renovating some of her own furniture.

SCALLOPS ON A JULIENNE OF VEGETABLES WITH A MOUSSELINE SAUCE

8 medium or 12 small scallops, cleaned
  (corals reserved)
60 ml (2 fl oz) Noilly Prat

Fish Stock:
1 celery stick
1 leek (white part only)
1 small onion
50 g (2 oz) mushrooms
15 ml (1 tbsp) clarified butter
60 ml (2 fl oz) dry white wine
60 ml (2 fl oz) Noilly Prat
450 g (1 lb) white fish bones
1 bouquet garni
salt and freshly ground white pepper

Vegetable Julienne:
1 large carrot
½ small celery stick
1 small leek (white part only)
1 courgette

Mousseline Sauce:
15 ml (1 tbsp) white wine vinegar
15 ml (1 tbsp) crushed white peppercorns
3 egg yolks, beaten
250 ml (9 oz) clarified butter, melted
salt
few drops of lemon juice
1.25 ml (¼ tsp) Dijon mustard, to taste
60 ml (4 tbsp) double cream, whipped

To prepare the fish stock, finely dice the vegetables. Heat the butter in a large pan, add the vegetables and sweat gently for 10 minutes, stirring occasionally. Deglaze the pan with the white wine and Noilly Prat, then add 300 ml (½ pint) water and the fish bones. Stir, then add the bouquet garni. Bring slowly to the boil and simmer gently for 20 minutes, skimming frequently. Strain through a muslin-lined sieve into a clean pan. Season well with salt and pepper.

To prepare the vegetable julienne, cut the vegetables into fine julienne strips, keeping each vegetable separate. Bring the fish stock to a simmer, then add the vegetables in the following order: carrot, celery, leek, and finally courgette. Poach briefly until soft, but retaining some bite. Drain, reserving the stock. Keep the julienne warm in a covered dish.

To make the mousseline sauce, put the wine vinegar, crushed peppercorns and 30 ml (2 tbsp) water in a small pan and boil to reduce to 15 ml (1 tbsp) liquid. Allow to cool. Strain into a heat-proof bowl and add 15 ml (1 tbsp) water. Put the bowl over a pan of hot but not boiling water. Add the egg yolks, whisking vigorously all the time. Continue to whisk until the mixture is thick and creamy.

Add the butter very slowly, whisking vigorously all the time. Season with salt to taste and add a few drops of lemon juice. Add enough mustard to give the sauce a slight piquancy. Keep warm for a few minutes if necessary over the pan of water, but make sure the water does not boil. Fold in the whipped cream just before serving.

To cook the scallops, heat the reserved fish stock in a pan, add the Noilly Prat and bring to a simmer. Add the scallops and poach gently for 2-3 minutes, turning them once. Drain and slice each scallop horizontally into three pieces.

To serve, place a little of the vegetable julienne on each warmed plate. Arrange the scallop slices on top and spoon some mousseline sauce over the scallops. Serve immediately.

Best End of Lamb in a Port and Rosemary Demi-glace Sauce

2 best ends of lamb, boned (bones and trimmings reserved)
1 rosemary stem
2 cloves garlic
120 ml (4 fl oz) red wine
15 ml (1 tbsp) olive oil
a little clarified butter
salt and freshly ground black pepper

Stock:

1.5 kg (3 lb) marrow or veal bones if available
bones and meat trimmings from the lamb
75 g (3 oz) clarified butter, melted
30 ml (2 tbsp) groundnut oil
4 carrots, roughly chopped
1 celery stick, roughly chopped
1 onion, chopped
125 g (4 oz) mushrooms, chopped
2 shallots, finely chopped
1 leek, roughly chopped
2 cloves garlic, finely chopped
225 g (8 oz) can tomatoes
250 ml (8 fl oz) white wine
2 thyme sprigs
1 parsley sprig
1 bay leaf
2 egg whites

Demi-glace:

2 rosemary sprigs
120 ml (4 fl oz) red wine
15 ml (1 tbsp) dried herbs de provence
6 black peppercorns
30 ml (1 fl oz) tawny port

To prepare the stock, put all the bones and meat trimmings in a roasting tin and brush with half of the butter. Roast in a preheated oven at 230°C (450°F) mark 8 for about 45 minutes until well coloured, turning the bones at least once and brushing with more butter.

Meanwhile, heat the oil in a very large pan or stock pot and add the vegetables and garlic. Sweat gently until soft and lightly coloured. Add the tomatoes, wine and herbs. Add the bones and deglaze the roasting tin with water. Fill the stock pot with water and simmer gently for 4-5 hours, skimming regularly. Discard bones. Strain the stock through a sieve into a clean pan, pressing the vegetables firmly.

Allow the stock to cool, then whisk in the 2 egg whites. Bring slowly to the boil and simmer for 10 minutes. The egg white will collect the sediment and form a froth on the surface, leaving a clear, sparkling stock below. Make a hole in the frothy layer and ladle the stock out. Strain through a muslin-lined sieve into a bowl. Draw off any fat from the surface.

To make the demi-glace, add the rosemary and red wine to the stock. Tie the herbs and peppercorns in a piece of muslin and add to the pan. Simmer the stock until it is reduced to about 300 ml (½ pint). Strain through a fine sieve into a clean pan. Add the port and continue to reduce the demi-glace, skimming if necessary, until only 150 ml (¼ pint) of completely clear, syrupy sauce remains.

To prepare the lamb, stud with tiny sprigs of rosemary and slivers of garlic. Mix the wine and oil together in a dish, add the meat and turn to coat. Leave to marinate for 2 hours, turning once.

Heat a little clarified butter in a small roasting dish in a preheated oven at 200°C (400°F) mark 6. Remove the meat from the marinade, discard the rosemary and garlic and pat dry with kitchen paper. Season with salt and pepper and place in the roasting dish. Roast in the oven for about 10 minutes until cooked but still pink inside. Wrap in foil and leave to rest in a warm place for 10-15 minutes.

To serve, reheat the demi-glace. Carve the lamb into fine slices and arrange on individual warmed plates on a pool of demi-glace. Garnish with rosemary.

SPINACH DARIOLES

900 g (2 lb) spinach
salt and freshly ground black pepper

Clean the spinach thoroughly and remove the coarse stems. Select 16 good leaves and heat these gently in a pan, with only the water clinging to the leaves after washing, until they wilt. Use to line 4 buttered ramekins, allowing the leaves to overhang the edges.

Cook the remaining spinach in two batches, without additional liquid, until wilted. Drain very thoroughly. Chop the cooked spinach finely and add salt and pepper to taste. Fill the ramekin dishes with the chopped spinach and fold the lining leaves over the top.

Place in a bain-marie (or roasting tin containing enough hot water to come halfway up the sides of the ramekins). Cover with a piece of buttered grease-proof paper and warm through in a preheated oven at 170°C (325°F) mark 3 for about 15 minutes.

SAUTÉ POTATOES

4 medium potatoes
salt and freshly ground black pepper
30-45 ml (2-3 tbsp) clarified butter
few drops of port

Cook the potatoes in their skins in boiling salted water until almost tender. Allow to cool, then slice thickly.

Heat the butter in a large frying pan and sauté the potatoes in batches, in one layer, until crisp and golden. Turn and cook the other side. Sprinkle with salt and pepper and the port. Drain on kitchen paper and keep warm while cooking the remainder. Serve immediately.

CELERIAC PURÉE IN FILO CASES

2 sheets of filo pastry
clarified butter, for brushing

Celeriac Purée:

1 celeriac
salt and freshly ground black pepper
15 ml (1 tbsp) double cream
paprika, for sprinkling

To make the filo pastry cases, brush 1 sheet of filo pastry with melted butter, lay the other sheet of pastry on top and brush with butter. Brush 4 individual tartlet tins with butter. Line each tin with the layered filo pastry, cutting to fit, and trim the edges. Bake in a preheated oven at 180°C (350°F) mark 4 for about 10 minutes until crisp.

To make the celeriac purée, peel the celeriac and cut into even-sized pieces. Cook in boiling salted water until tender. Drain, then purée in a food processor or blender. Pass through a sieve into a bowl and beat in the cream. Season with salt and pepper to taste.

To serve, warm the pastry cases in the oven if necessary. Spoon some celeriac purée into each one and sprinkle with a little paprika.

CARROT RIBBONS

3 carrots
knob of butter
2.5 ml (½ tsp) ground coriander
salt and freshly ground black pepper

Peel the carrots and using the vegetable peeler, shave long ribbons from the carrots. Put the butter, coriander, salt and pepper into a pan with a little water. Add the carrot ribbons and cook gently until tender and glazed with butter. Serve immediately.

PROVENÇAL LAVENDER HONEY AND GINGER ICE CREAM

Using an ice-cream maker gives this ice cream a very light texture. If you do not own one, whisk the ice cream 2 or 3 times during freezing to break down the ice crystals.

4 egg yolks
25 g (1 oz) caster sugar
300 ml (½ pint) single cream
6 pieces preserved stem ginger in syrup, finely chopped
15 ml (1 tbsp) ginger syrup (from the stem ginger jar)
30 ml (2 tbsp) provençal lavender honey
300 ml (½ pint) double cream

Chocolate Sauce:
125 g (4 oz) dark chocolate, in pieces
75 ml (2½ fl oz) milk
15 ml (1 tbsp) double cream
15 g (½ oz) caster sugar
15 g (½ oz) butter

Raspberry Coulis:
125 g (4 oz) fresh or frozen raspberries
lemon juice, to taste
icing sugar, to taste

Whisk the egg yolks and sugar together in a bowl until pale and creamy. Heat the cream until almost boiling, then pour on to the egg mixture, stirring. Strain back into the pan and cook very gently, stirring constantly, until the custard thickens slightly, just enough to coat the back of a spoon. Remove from the heat and stir in the chopped ginger, ginger syrup and honey. Allow to cool.

Whip the double cream lightly and stir into the cold custard. Place in an ice-cream maker and freeze for approximately 40 minutes. Turn into a freezer-proof container and store in the freezer, but transfer to the refrigerator about 15 minutes before serving to soften.

To make the chocolate sauce, melt the chocolate in a bowl over a pan of hot water. In a small pan, gently heat the milk, cream and sugar together, then bring to the boil, stirring. Pour over the melted chocolate, then return to the pan. Bring to the boil and simmer for 15 seconds. Remove from the heat and whisk in the butter.

To make the coulis, purée the raspberries in a blender or food processor with a little water if necessary. Pass through a sieve and flavour with a little lemon juice or icing sugar as required.

Serve the ice cream scooped into brandy snap baskets, with the raspberry coulis and warm or cold chocolate sauce.

BRANDY SNAP BASKETS

25 g (1 oz) butter
30 ml (2 tbsp) granulated sugar
15 ml (1 tbsp) golden syrup
30 ml (2 tbsp) plain flour
2.5 ml (½ tsp) ground ginger
pinch of salt
12 ml (½ tbsp) brandy
12 ml (½ tbsp) lemon juice

Melt the butter, sugar and syrup together in a small pan over a low heat. Remove from the heat and beat in the rest of the ingredients.

Place teaspoonfuls of the mixture on a baking sheet lined with non-stick baking parchment, spreading the mixture into even-sized circles, and leaving plenty of space between them for spreading. Bake in a preheated oven at 180°C (350°F) mark 4 for 6-8 minutes until golden brown.

Let cool for 20 seconds only, then drape each brandy snap over an upturned greased ramekin dish, moulding the sides firmly to make a basket. Allow to cool, then remove.

The First
Semi-Final
Brian Tompkins • Richard Kuch • Rachel Southall

Winner

Brian Tompkins' Menu

Starter
Marinated Halibut Fillets with a Sherry and Shallot Dressing,
nestled on a Symphony of Seaweed

Main Course
Pan-fried Saddle of Wild Rabbit on a Russet Bowl
with a Herb Mustard Sauce and Forest Mushrooms
Sweet Potato and Beetroot Gâteaux

Dessert
Lavender Baked Figs on Brioche Toasts, served with
Cassis Glacage and Blackberry Confiture
"A fabulous dessert... and so clever" Jean Marsh

MARINATED HALIBUT FILLETS WITH A SHERRY AND SHALLOT DRESSING, NESTLED ON A SYMPHONY OF SEAWEED

If halibut is unobtainable, use another good firm white fish, such as cod or sole. Whichever fish you use, it must be *very* fresh.

225-250 g (8-9 oz) middle-cut halibut fillet

Marinade:
10 ml (2 tsp) mixed coloured peppercorns
300 ml (½ pint) sherry vinegar
juice and finely zested rind of 1 lemon
4 shallots, finely chopped
15 ml (1 tbsp) clear honey
15 ml (1 tbsp) chopped parsley
salt, to taste
5 ml (1 tsp) caster sugar

To Serve:
handful of Japanese dried seaweed
a little extra-virgin olive oil
chicory leaves, to garnish

Cut the halibut across the grain into thin slices about 5 mm (¼ inch) thick. Place in a shallow dish.

Roughly crush half of the peppercorns; leave the rest whole. Mix all the marinade ingredients together in a bowl, then pour over the fish. Leave to marinate and effectively 'cook' in the acids of the marinade for approximately 1½ hours, turning the fish occasionally to ensure even 'cooking'.

Reconstitute the seaweed by soaking in cold water to cover for about 10 minutes. Drain well. Just before serving remove the fish from the marinade.

To serve, pile the seaweed in the centre of the serving plates and arrange 3 slices of fish radially on top. Pour some of the marinade around the seaweed, then drizzle with a little olive oil. Garnish with chicory leaves.

SWEET POTATO AND BEETROOT GÂTEAUX

To mould these gâteaux you need tall metal or plastic heat-resistant rings, about 10 cm (4 inches) high and 6 cm (2 ½ inches) in diameter. I use a piece of pipe – cut to size – obtained from my local DIY store!

3 sweet potatoes
½ celeriac
1 cooked beetroot (preferably from the garden)
40 g (1½ oz) smoked butter or unsalted butter
salt and pepper
1 bunch of spring onions, sliced into rounds
5 ml (1 tsp) finely grated orange rind
chives, to garnish

Peel and grate the sweet potatoes, celeriac and beetroot. Melt 25 g (1 oz) of the butter in a pan, add the sweet potatoes and cook gently for about 10 minutes until softened. Add the celeriac and cook for a further 5 minutes. Season with salt and pepper; set aside.

Melt the remaining butter in another pan and gently sweat the spring onions for a few minutes until softened. Add the beetroot and orange rind and heat through for 1-2 minutes. Season with salt and pepper.

To assemble each gâteau, place the tall ring or piece of pipe (see above) in the centre of the warmed serving plate. Put a heaped tablespoon of the potato into the ring and tamp down with the base of a wine glass. Add a heaped tablespoon of beetroot mixture and press down, then top with another layer of potato, pressing down firmly. Gently slide the ring off leaving the gâteau on the plate. Repeat to make 4 gâteaux in total. Garnish with chives to serve.

PAN-FRIED SADDLE OF WILD RABBIT ON A RUSSET BOWL WITH A FINE HERB MUSTARD SAUCE AND FOREST MUSHROOMS

2 young wild or farmed rabbits, each
    weighing about 1.25 kg (2½ lb)
2 russet apples
40 g (1½ oz) clarified butter
salt and freshly ground black pepper

Stock:
1 leek, chopped
1 carrot, chopped
1 onion, chopped
1 celery stick, chopped
2-3 mushrooms, chopped
120 ml (4 fl oz) dry sherry
1 bouquet garni

Sauce:
300 ml (½ pint) whipping cream
60 ml (2 fl oz) dry sherry
60 ml (2 fl oz) Noilly Prat
10 ml (2 tsp) fine herb green mustard

To Garnish:
125 g (4 oz) wild mushrooms, sliced
dash of dry sherry

Carefully remove the saddles and hind legs from each rabbit, then bone out the thighs. Remove the forelegs. Reserve the carcasses and trimmings.

To prepare the stock, break the rabbit carcasses into pieces and chop the trimmings. Place in a stock pot or large flameproof dish and cook in a preheated oven at 200°C (400°F) mark 6 for 10 minutes, do not allow to brown. Add the chopped vegetables, stir well and cook for 10-15 minutes to soften them.

Transfer to the top of the cooker and deglaze with the sherry, stirring to scrape up the sediment. Add 900 ml (1½ pints) water, and the bouquet garni. Cover and simmer for about 1 hour.

Strain the stock through a fine sieve, return to the clean pan and boil to reduce to about 300 ml (½ pint) stock.

To make the russet bowls; cut each apple in half crosswise through the centre to give 4 bowls. Scoop out the cores and enough flesh to hollow out each 'bowl'. Cut a sliver off the base of each bowl so it stands level.

Heat 25 g (1 oz) clarified butter in a large frying pan and fry the apple bowls, cut-side down for 3 minutes. Season the rabbit legs, then add to the pan and fry over a high heat to seal on all sides. Transfer to a roasting tin and cook in the oven at 200°C (400°F) mark 6 for about 10 minutes; the meat should still be a little pink. Cover with foil and leave to rest for 5-10 minutes.

Meanwhile reduce the cream for the sauce by boiling to 150 ml (¼ pint).

Season the saddles of rabbit, then add to the frying pan and cook, turning, over a high heat for 3-4 minutes. Remove, cover with foil and leave to rest while making the sauce.

To make the sauce, deglaze the pan with the sherry and Noilly Prat, stirring to scrape up the sediment. Stir in the mustard, stock and reduced cream and reheat, stirring until smooth. Strain the sauce through a fine sieve. Check the seasoning and keep warm.

To prepare the garnish, fry the wild mushrooms in the remaining butter until tender. Season with salt and pepper, add a dash of sherry and immediately remove from the heat. Keep warm.

To serve, place a russet bowl in the centre of each warmed serving plate. Cut the rabbit thigh meat into bite-sized pieces. Slice the saddles diagonally. Place a foreleg in each russet bowl. Arrange the thigh and saddle meat around this. Pour on the sauce and garnish with the wild mushrooms. Serve with the vegetable gâteaux.

LAVENDER BAKED FIGS ON BRIOCHE TOASTS, WITH CASSIS GLACAGE AND BLACKBERRY CONFITURE

To make the lavender sugar, simply add a good handful of dried lavender flowers to a 450 g (1 lb) jar of caster sugar and leave in your storecupboard to use as you would any flavoured sugar. Lavender sugar imparts a delicious flavour to custard and makes a refreshing change from vanilla.

Ready-made cassis purée is sold in cartons but it is not widely available. If you are unable to buy it, simply make your own blackcurrant purée.

8 fresh figs
125 g (4 oz) lavender sugar

Blackberry Confiture:

60 ml (4 tbsp) caster sugar
½ glass crème de mure, or crème de cassis
30 blackberries

Cassis Glacage:

1 egg yolk
30 ml (2 tbsp) caster sugar
150 ml (¼ pint) whipping cream
15 ml (1 tbsp) cassis purée (approximately)

To Serve:

8 slices brioche, each 1 cm (½ inch) thick

First make the confiture, dissolve the sugar in the liqueur in a pan over a low heat, then boil to reduce to a thick syrup. Add the blackberries and cook gently for about 2 minutes only, until softened but still retaining their shape. Remove the blackberries with a slotted spoon and set aside on a plate. Reserve the syrup.

To make the cassis glacage, whisk the egg yolk with the sugar and cream until thick, then fold in enough cassis purée to give a rich lilac colour. Set aside.

To prepare the syrup for the figs, put the lavender sugar (including flowers) and 100 ml (3½ fl oz) water in a pan over a low heat to dissolve the sugar. Increase the heat and boil to reduce the syrup slightly. Add the figs and shake the pan to coat the figs in the syrup. Transfer to an ovenproof dish, cover and place in a preheated oven at 200°C (400°F) mark 6 for 5-10 minutes to heat through. Remove from the oven and set aside.

Cut the brioche slices into rounds, then brown lightly on both sides under a hot grill.

To serve, pour or spread about a tablespoon of the glacage onto one side of an individual flameproof plate. Place under a very hot grill and watch carefully. First the egg will cook which sets the glacarge, then almost immediately the top will begin to brown. As soon as you have a nice brown topping, remove before it burns. Repeat with the other servings.

Make a cross-cut in the top of each fig and push up from the bottom so the 'petals' open out. Place a fig on each brioche toast, next to the cassis glacage and spoon over any spare syrup. Place a spoonful of blackberry confiture syrup and a pile of blackberries on each plate. Serve immediately.

THE FIRST
SEMI-FINAL
BRIAN TOMPKINS • RICHARD KUCH • RACHEL SOUTHALL

RICHARD KUCH'S MENU

STARTER
Fillets of Sole with Avocado and Basil

MAIN COURSE
Lamb en Croûte, with a Port and Orange Sauce
Celeriac Mousse

DESSERT
Vanilla Pears with an Almond Filling, served with
a Chocolate Sauce

"SO BEAUTIFULLY MADE. THE MARZIPAN FILLING WAS
A NICE SURPRISE" LOYD

"AS AN ENSEMBLE THIS IS A WONDERFUL MENU" LOYD

FILLETS OF SOLE WITH AVOCADO AND BASIL

2 shallots, chopped
8 Dover sole fillets, each about 125 g (4 oz)
salt and freshly ground black pepper
475 ml (16 fl oz) fish stock
125 ml (4 fl oz) double cream
2 large avocados
15 ml (1 tbsp) coarsely chopped basil leaves
15 g (½ oz) butter, chilled and diced
lemon juice, for brushing

To Garnish:
1 tomato, seeded and diced
6 small basil sprigs

Grease an ovenproof baking dish, measuring about 23 x 15 cm (9 x 6 inches) with butter. Sprinkle the chopped shallots evenly in the dish.

Season the fish with salt and pepper, then lightly flatten the fillets and tie each into a loose knot, or fold over to make a triangle. Arrange in the baking dish.

Bring the fish stock to a simmer in a pan, then pour over the fish. Cover the dish and bake in a preheated oven at 200°C (400°F) mark 6 for 8-12 minutes, until firm to the touch. Keep the sole fillets warm.

Strain the cooking liquid into a saucepan and boil to reduce to 250 ml (8 fl oz). Add the cream and reduce again by about a quarter.

Pour the sauce into a food processor or blender. Peel and chop one of the avocados, discarding the stone. With the machine running, add the avocado, a piece at a time, together with the basil until all incorporated – processing to a purée.

With the machine running, add the butter, a piece at a time. Check the seasoning. Strain the sauce through a fine sieve, if necessary. Reheat gently.

To serve, halve, peel and stone the remaining avocado and cut into slices. Brush with a little lemon juice to prevent discolouration. Arrange a fan of avocado slices on each serving plate. Arrange 2 sole fillets on each plate and coat with the sauce. Garnish with tomato and basil. Serve immediately.

LAMB EN CROÛTE, WITH A PORT AND ORANGE SAUCE

The cooking time for this dish is critical. The pastry needs to be crisp and golden brown, while the enclosed lamb fillet should be pink and tender.

25 g (1 oz) unsalted butter
2 fillets of lamb, each about 400 g (14 oz)
salt and freshly ground black pepper
18 large spinach leaves
450 g (1 lb) ready-made puff pastry
beaten egg, to glaze

Port and Orange Sauce:
150 ml (¼ pint) veal stock
150 ml (¼ pint) dry red wine
juice of 2 oranges
juice of ½ lemon
30 ml (2 tbsp) redcurrant jelly
1 shallot, finely chopped
1 clove garlic
2.5 ml (½ tsp) chopped fresh root ginger
1 thyme sprig
1 bay leaf
60 ml (4 tbsp) ruby port
65 g (2½ oz) unsalted butter, chilled and diced
salt and freshly ground pepper

Heat the butter in a frying pan, add the lamb fillets and cook over a high heat for 2 minutes, turning to seal on all sides. Remove from the pan, season with salt and pepper and allow to cool.

Blanch the spinach leaves in boiling water for 5-7 seconds only, refresh in cold water, then drain. Lay out the spinach leaves in two lines, the same length as the lamb fillets. Lay a lamb fillet on each line of spinach and wrap the spinach leaves around each piece of lamb to enclose.

Cut the pastry in half. Roll out each piece to a rectangle and place a spinach-wrapped fillet in the centre. Brush the edges of the pastry with beaten egg and wrap each fillet in pastry, pressing the edges to seal. Place seam-side down on a baking sheet and leave to rest at room temperature for about 30 minutes.

Meanwhile to make the sauce, put all the ingredients, except the port, butter and seasoning, in a pan. Bring to the boil and boil to reduce by three quarters, skimming occasionally. Strain through a fine sieve, then return to the pan and reheat. Add the port and simmer for a few minutes.

To cook the lamb, brush the pastry with beaten egg and bake in a preheated oven at 200°C (400°F) mark 6 for 15-20 minutes, until the pastry is crisp and golden brown.

To finish the sauce, whisk in the butter a piece at a time on and off the heat, making sure each piece is thoroughly incorporated before adding the next. Season with salt and pepper to taste.

To serve, cut the lamb into slices and arrange on warmed serving plates. Spoon on the sauce and serve at once, with the celeriac mousse.

CELERIAC MOUSSE

1 celeriac
25 g (1 oz) unsalted butter
1 shallot, finely chopped
2 sage leaves
1 litre (1¾ pints) vegetable stock
60 ml (4 tbsp) double cream
1 egg
2 egg yolks
salt and freshly ground white pepper

Peel the celeriac and cut into 2.5 cm (1 inch) cubes. Cook in a large pan of boiling water for 5 minutes. Drain thoroughly.

Melt the butter in a pan, add the shallot and cook until soft. Add the celeriac, sage and vegetable stock. Bring to the boil, cover and simmer for 15-18 minutes until tender. Drain, reserving the liquid. Return the liquid to the pan and boil to reduce to about 200 ml (⅓ pint).

Put the celeriac mixture in a blender or food processor and process with enough of the reduced stock to yield a smooth purée, the consistency of a thick cream. Turn into a bowl and fold in the cream, whole egg and egg yolks. Pass through a fine sieve into a clean bowl. Taste and adjust the seasoning.

Butter 4 ramekins or dariole moulds and fill with the celeriac mixture. Cover the tops with buttered foil and place in a bain-marie (roasting tin containing enough hot water to come halfway up the sides of the moulds). Cook in a preheated oven at 180°C (350°F) mark 4 for 20 minutes or until the mousses are firm and a skewer inserted into the centre comes out clean. Turn out onto warmed plates to serve.

VANILLA PEARS WITH AN ALMOND FILLING AND CHOCOLATE SAUCE

175 g (6 oz) granulated sugar
juice of ½ lemon
1 vanilla pod
4 dessert pears

Almond Filling:
15 ml (1 tbsp) Grand Marnier
75 g (3 oz) white marzipan
25 g (1 oz) amaretti biscuits, crushed

Chocolate Sauce:
40 g (1½ oz) caster sugar
100 g (3½ oz) plain chocolate, chopped
20 ml (4 tsp) whipping cream
15 ml (1 tbsp) kirsch

To Decorate:
15-30 (1-2 tbsp) yogurt
25 g (1 oz) flaked almonds, toasted

Dissolve the sugar in 900 ml (1½ pints) water in a saucepan over low heat. Add the lemon juice and vanilla; bring to a simmer. Peel the pears and scoop out the cores with a melon baller, from the bases. Place the pears in the syrup. Cover with a circle of greaseproof paper and poach gently for 20-25 minutes or until tender. Leave to cool in the syrup.

To prepare the filling, work the Grand Marnier into the marzipan until smooth. Mix in the crushed amaretti biscuits.

To make the chocolate sauce, dissolve the sugar in 75 ml (5 tbsp) water in a saucepan over a low heat. Bring to the boil, then remove from the heat. Add the chocolate, stirring until dissolved, then stir in the cream and kirsch. Allow to cool.

Drain the pears and push a little filling into each one, through the base. Halve lengthwise and arrange on serving plates. Surround with chocolate sauce, dot with yogurt and feather with a skewer. Decorate with almonds.

THE FIRST
SEMI-FINAL

BRIAN TOMPKINS • RICHARD KUCH • RACHEL SOUTHALL

RACHEL SOUTHALL'S MENU

STARTER

Cream of Watercress Soup

"THIS IS A LOVELY SOUP. FRESHNESS AND CLEANNESS ARE
VERY IMPORTANT IN WATERCRESS SOUP" RAYMOND BLANC

MAIN COURSE

*Turbot Steak with Pink Grapefruit
and Asparagus in a Sauternes Sauce
Steamed New Potatoes
Leek Julienne in Butter
Carrot Julienne*

"THE TURBOT WAS ABSOLUTELY AMAZING... THE GRAPEFRUIT
WAS ESSENTIAL THERE" RAYMOND BLANC

DESSERT

Pears in Pastry Lattice, with Lime Butterscotch Sauce

"I CAN'T IMAGINE A BETTER PUDDING THAN THAT... THE SAUCE
WAS IMMACULATE" LOYD

CREAM OF WATERCRESS SOUP

4 bunches of watercress
50 g (2 oz) butter
1 onion, finely chopped
2 cloves garlic, crushed
50 g (2 oz) plain flour
600 ml (1 pint) chicken stock
600 ml (1 pint) milk
salt and freshly ground black pepper
1.25 ml (¼ tsp) freshly grated nutmeg
juice of ½ lemon
150 ml (¼ pint) single cream
watercress sprigs, to garnish

Trim the watercress, discarding the tough stalks, then chop roughly.

Melt the butter in a saucepan and gently fry the onion and garlic until soft. Reduce the heat and stir in the flour. Gradually add the stock and milk, stirring all the time. Stir in the chopped watercress, salt, pepper, nutmeg and lemon juice. Simmer gently for 5 minutes. Don't worry if it appears to separate at this point!

Purée the soup in a blender or food processor until smooth, then return to the clean pan. Reheat gently; do not allow to boil. Stir in the cream and adjust the seasoning.

Pour the soup into warmed individual bowls and garnish each serving with a sprig of watercress. Serve immediately.

TURBOT STEAKS WITH PINK GRAPEFRUIT AND ASPARAGUS

4 portions of turbot fillet, each 150 g (5 oz),
  skin removed
a little plain flour, for coating
40 g (1½ oz) butter
salt and freshly ground black pepper
1 pink grapefruit
16 green asparagus tips
150 ml (¼ pint) vegetable stock or water

Sauce:

50 ml (2 fl oz) fish stock
50 ml (2 fl oz) vegetable stock
12 peppercorns
10 g (½ oz) shallot, finely chopped
50 ml (2 fl oz) Sauternes
25 ml (1 fl oz) double cream
100 g (3½ oz) unsalted butter, chilled and
  diced

Dust the portions of turbot with a little flour and mark a lattice design on each one, using a red hot skewer. Melt 25 g (1 oz) of the butter and brush over the fish. Season with salt and pepper and set aside.

Peel and segment the grapefruit over a bowl to catch the juice, discarding all white pith and pips. Set aside the best 12 segments. Squeeze the juice from the remainder if necessary to give 50 ml (2 fl oz) juice.

To make the sauce, place the fish and vegetable stocks, peppercorns, shallot, Sauternes and reserved grapefruit juice in a saucepan and bring to the boil, then boil to reduce by half. Add the cream and reduce by half again. Stir in the butter, a little at a time. Pass the sauce through a fine sieve and check the seasoning. Keep warm.

Place the turbot, lattice-side down on a grill rack and grill under a medium heat for 4 minutes. Turn each portion over, brush with melted butter and grill for 4 minutes.

Meanwhile cook the asparagus briefly in boiling vegetable stock or water, then drain and toss in the reserved 15 g (½ oz) butter. Season with salt and pepper. Warm the pink grapefruit segments by simply placing them on a hot plate.

Transfer the turbot to warmed serving plates and arrange the grapefruit segments and asparagus tips on the plates. Pour a little sauce beside each turbot portion. Serve immediately, with steamed new potatoes, julienne of leeks in butter and carrot julienne.

PEARS IN PASTRY LATTICE WITH LIME BUTTERSCOTCH SAUCE

To make the pastry lattice for this dessert you will need a lattice roller. This is a plastic or perspex cylinder with 'blades' set in it. As you roll the lattice roller over the pastry it cuts slits in the pastry. When the pastry is lifted from the work surface these slits open up to form the lattice. You can buy an inexpensive lattice roller from a kitchen shop or mail order cookware supplier.

2 ripe, firm pears
225 g (8 oz) puff pastry
a little milk, to glaze

Sugar Syrup:
250 g (9 oz) caster sugar
25 ml (1 fl oz) lemon juice

Frangipane:
60 g (2¼ oz) unsalted butter, softened
60 g (2¼ oz) caster sugar
1 egg, beaten
60 g (2¼ oz) ground almonds
15 g (½ oz) plain flour

Sauce:
75 g (3 oz) caster sugar
50 ml (2 fl oz) liquid glucose
juice of 1 lime
250 ml (8 fl oz) double cream

To make the sugar syrup, put the sugar, lemon juice and 500 ml (16 fl oz) water in a saucepan and heat gently until the sugar is dissolved, then bring to the boil. Peel, halve and core the pears, then add to the syrup and poach for about 20 minutes until tender. Remove from the syrup and leave to cool on a plate.

To make the frangipane, put all the ingredients in a bowl and whisk together thoroughly using an electric whisk until smooth.

Roll out half of the puff pastry thinly on a lightly floured surface and cut 4 pear shapes, about 1 cm (½ inch) larger all round than the pears. Roll out the other half of the pastry, then roll with the lattice roller to make your pastry lattice.

Spread a small amount of frangipane on each pear-shaped piece of pastry, leaving a 1 cm (½ inch) border. Place a pear on top and brush the pastry edges with a little milk. Cut a piece of lattice pastry to fit over each pear and carefully position over the pears. Press the pastry edges together to seal and trim to neaten.

Place on a lightly greased baking tray and brush with milk to glaze. Cut 4 small leaves from the pastry trimmings, brush with milk and place on the baking tray. Cook in a preheated oven at 190°C (375°F) mark 5 for about 10 minutes until the pastry is crisp and golden brown.

To make the sauce, put the sugar and glucose in a saucepan with 25 ml (1 fl oz) water over a low heat until the sugar is dissolved. Add the lime juice and cream, bring to the boil and boil for 1 minute.

To serve, place a lattice pear on each warmed serving plate and decorate with a small pastry leaf. Pour the sauce around each pear and serve immediately.

THE SECOND
SEMI-FINAL
ROSS BURDEN • TONY DAVIS • HELEN WELLER

WINNER

ROSS BURDEN'S MENU

STARTER

Lightly Poached Oysters with Trompettes

MAIN COURSE

Roast Rabbit on Watercress with a Port Sauce
Roast Shallots
Spinach Terrine with Rabbit Livers
Game Chips

"THE ROAST RABBIT WAS UTTERLY SENSATIONAL" STEPHEN FRY

"IT LOOKED LOVELY. BRILLIANT SAUCE. I HAVE NEVER SEEN A SAUCE
QUITE THAT BROWN" JOSCELINE DIMBLEBY

DESSERT

Green Figs with Chartreuse en Papillote

LIGHTLY POACHED OYSTERS WITH TROMPETTES

I used Colchester rock oysters for this starter, as they have a very good flavour.

1 cucumber
salt and freshly ground black pepper
24 oysters, scrubbed clean
150 g (5 oz) unsalted butter, chilled and
   diced
2 large shallots, finely chopped
15 ml (1 tbsp) dry white wine
5 ml (1 tsp) white wine vinegar
5 ml (1 tsp) single cream
squeeze of lime juice (optional)
15 ml (1 tbsp) oil
24 horn of plenty mushrooms (trompettes),
   cleaned
pinch of paprika (optional)

Peel the cucumber, reserving about 50 g (2 oz) of the peelings. Prepare a garnish of small lozenges, about 1 cm x 5 mm (¾ x ¼ inch), from the cucumber flesh. Sprinkle these with a little salt and freeze for 1 hour. Finely chop the cucumber peelings. Open the oysters and drain, reserving the juices; clean thoroughly.

Melt 5 ml (1 tsp) of the butter in a small saucepan, add the chopped cucumber peelings and shallots and sweat gently until softened. Add the wine and vinegar and allow to reduce until only 5 ml (1 tsp) of liquid remains. Reduce the heat to a minimum, then add the cream and 10 ml (2 tsp) of the reserved oyster juices.

Gradually whisk in the butter, a piece at a time, on and off the heat, until it is all incorporated. Purée in a blender or food processor until smooth, then pass through a fine sieve into a small jug. Season with salt and pepper, and add a squeeze of lime juice if desired. Keep warm by placing the jug in a bowl of warm water.

Rinse the cucumber garnish and warm gently in a bowl over a pan of hot water.

Heat the oil in a sauté pan, add the mushrooms and sauté gently until softened.

Heat the rest of the oyster juices in a shallow pan. When the juices are very hot, add the oysters and poach for 3 seconds only. Remove with a slotted spoon and drain.

To assemble, place a spoonful of the beurre blanc in the centre of each warmed serving plate and arrange 6 oysters on top. Interleave the oysters with trompettes and garnish with the cucumber lozenges and a pinch of paprika if desired.

ROAST RABBIT ON WATERCRESS WITH A PORT SAUCE

The rabbit livers are reserved for the Spinach Terrine, which is served as an accompaniment.

2 domestic rabbits, each about 900 g (2 lb), jointed into saddles and hind legs; carcasses, kidneys and livers reserved
20 ml (4 tsp) oil
50 g (2 oz) butter
12 shallots
120 ml (4 fl oz) port
500 ml (18 fl oz) white chicken or veal stock
450 g (1 lb) watercress leaves (stalks removed)
salt and freshly ground pepper
4 chervil sprigs, to garnish

Roughly chop the rabbit carcasses. Heat the oil and 15 g (½ oz) of the butter in a heavy-based frying pan and sear the rabbit joints over a high heat, turning to seal on all sides. Remove from the pan and repeat with the carcasses.

Transfer the rabbit joints and carcasses to a roasting tin and cook in a preheated oven at 220°C (425 °F) mark 7 for 12 minutes. Remove the saddles to a warmed dish, cover and keep warm. Return the roasting tin to the oven and cook the legs and carcasses for a further 10 minutes. At the same time, roast the shallots in a separate tin with 15 g (½ oz) melted butter for about 10 minutes. Transfer the rabbit legs to the dish containing the saddles; keep warm.

Drain off the oil from the roasting tin, retaining the bones in the tin. Place on top of the cooker over a moderate heat and add the port to deglaze, stirring to scrape up the sediment. Boil to reduce by half, then add the stock and reduce by half again. Strain through a muslin-lined sieve into a clean pan; check the seasoning and keep warm.

Melt the remaining butter in small pan and cook the watercress leaves for 2-3 minutes until wilted. Remove with a slotted spoon; keep warm. Halve the rabbit kidneys, add to the pan and flash-fry briefly until browned on both sides, but still pink in the middle. Remove from the pan.

To serve, carve the rabbit saddles into slices. Place a bed of watercress on each serving plate and arrange the sliced rabbit and a leg on each portion. Garnish with the roasted shallots, kidneys and chervil sprigs. Pour the sauce around the watercress. Serve at once.

SPINACH TERRINE WITH RABBIT LIVERS

reserved livers from 2 rabbits
500 g (1 lb 2 oz) young spinach leaves
15 ml (1 tbsp) olive oil
200 g (7 oz) cooked white rice
2 eggs, lightly beaten
2.5 ml (½ tsp) freshly grated nutmeg
10 ml (2 tsp) freshly grated Parmesan cheese
salt and freshly ground black pepper

Clean and trim the rabbit livers, then cut into small even-sized pieces. Clean the spinach thoroughly, remove the stalks, then steam briefly until tender. Chop roughly and drain thoroughly.

Heat the oil in a frying pan and flash-fry the liver pieces over a high heat for about 30 seconds. Transfer to a large bowl and add the rice, eggs, nutmeg, cheese and seasoning. Stir well, then add the spinach and mix until evenly combined.

Turn into a greased 450 g (1 lb) loaf tin, spreading the mixture evenly. Place in a roasting tin half-filled with hot water. Bake in a preheated oven at 200 °C (400°F) mark 6 for about 30 minutes, until a skewer inserted into the centre comes out clean. Carefully turn out onto a warm plate and cut into slices to serve.

Note: When the terrine is ready it will be set, while the livers remain pink inside.

GREEN FIGS WITH CHARTREUSE EN PAPILLOTE

For the papillotes, you will need 4 large circles of non-stick baking parchment, each about 30 cm (12 inches) in diameter.

8 figs
1 large banana
20 ml (4 tsp) sugar
20 ml (4 tsp) unsalted butter
20 ml (4 tsp) green Chartreuse liqueur
melted butter, for brushing

Cut the tips off the figs, then make a cross-cut through the top of each one. Cut the banana into slices on the diagonal. Cut 4 circles of non-stick baking parchment, each 30 cm (12 inches) in diameter.

Arrange the banana slices on one half of each circle and sit the figs on top. Sprinkle with the sugar, dot with butter and drizzle over the liqueur. Brush the other half of the paper circles with water to moisten. Brush the edges of the circles with melted butter, then bring the moistened halves over the filling and press the edges together.

To seal each parcel, starting at one end of the semi-circle, fold the edges over to form a series of overlapping tucks. To ensure the pleats do not unroll during cooking, insert a strip of foil into each pleat. Bake in a preheated oven at 220°C (425°F) mark 7 for 6 minutes.

Serve immediately, accompanied by whipped cream flavoured with a little green Chartreuse if desired. Let your guests open their own parcels to reveal the contents!

THE SECOND
SEMI-FINAL
ROSS BURDEN • TONY DAVIS • HELEN WELLER

TONY DAVIS' MENU

STARTER

Chicken Consommé with Fresh Vegetables and
Vermouth topped with Puff Pastry

"IT MAY LOOK A GIMMICK, BUT IT ISN'T AT ALL.
IT'S FABULOUS" LOYD

MAIN COURSE

Turbans of Salmon and Sole, served with a
Watercress Sauce
Creamed Potatoes

DESSERT

Chocolate Gâteau

"EXQUISITE!" LOYD

CHICKEN CONSOMMÉ WITH FRESH VEGETABLES AND VERMOUTH TOPPED WITH PUFF PASTRY

60 ml (4 tbsp) dry white vermouth
600 ml (1 pint) well-flavoured hot chicken stock
125 g (4 oz) boneless chicken breast
25 g (1 oz) chicken liver pâté
25 g (1 oz) carrot
25 g (1 oz) onion
25 g (1 oz) celery
25 g (1 oz) mushrooms
15 ml (1 tbsp) unsalted butter
salt and freshly ground black pepper
400 g (14 oz) packet puff pastry
beaten egg yolk, to glaze

Divide the vermouth and hot chicken stock between individual ovenproof soup tureens. Cut the chicken breast into 5 mm (¼ inch) dice. Cut the chicken liver pâté into similar dice.

Finely dice the vegetables. Melt the butter in a small sauté pan and gently sauté the vegetables in the butter for about 5 minutes until softened. Divide the sautéed vegetables, chicken and pâté evenly between the soup bowls.

Roll out the pastry thinly on a lightly floured surface and cut 4 rounds, about 15 cm (6 inches) in diameter, to fit the tops of the soup tureens as lids. Carefully position a puff pastry round on each bowl, sealing the edges with beaten egg yolk.

Brush the pastry with beaten egg yolk to glaze. Bake in a preheated oven at 220°C (425°F) mark 7 for about 18-20 minutes until the pastry is well risen and golden brown. Serve immediately.

TURBANS OF SALMON AND SOLE, SERVED WITH A WATERCRESS SAUCE

Either fillet the fish yourself or get your fish-monger to do so for you, but remember to ask for the bones, heads and trimmings which you will need for the fumet.

Turbans:
8 small salmon fillets
8 small sole fillets
salt and freshly ground white pepper
25 g (1 oz) butter, melted

Mousseline:
225 g (8 oz) mixed white fish fillets (bream, whiting, haddock, etc)
1 egg white, size 2
250 ml (8 fl oz) double cream
25 g (1 oz) pistachio nuts, chopped

Fish Fumet:
450 g (1 lb) fish bones, heads and trimmings
1 onion, chopped
1 carrot, chopped
1 leek, chopped
1 bouquet garni
250 ml (8 fl oz) dry white wine

Watercress Sauce:
25 g (1 oz) butter
25 g (1 oz) plain flour
600 ml (1 pint) fish fumet
½ bunch watercress

To prepare the mousseline, purée the white fish in a food processor until smooth. Add the egg white and process briefly until evenly blended. Transfer to a pyrex bowl, cover the surface closely with cling film. Place in a large bowl containing ice and refrigerate for 1 hour. Uncover and gradually work in the cream. Fold in the pistachio nuts and season with salt. Cover and refrigerate until required.

To prepare the fish fumet, put the fish bones, heads and trimmings in a large saucepan with the vegetables. Add 600 ml (1 pint) water, the bouquet garni and white wine. Bring to the boil, cover and simmer gently for 20 minutes. Strain through a fine sieve and check the seasoning. Measure 600 ml (1 pint) for the watercress sauce.

To prepare the turbans, brush 4 individual baba moulds or dariole moulds with melted butter. Season the salmon and sole fillets and use to line the moulds: alternate the fillets and allow them to overhang the edges of the moulds by about 2.5 cm (1 inch). Pack the mousseline into the moulds and fold the overhanging fillets over the mousseline to enclose.

Cover each mould with a circle of greaseproof paper (cut to fit). Place on a wire rack in an ovenproof dish and pour enough hot water into the dish to come halfway up the sides of the moulds. Cook in a preheated oven at 170°C (325°F) mark 3 for 35-40 minutes until the turbans are set and springy to the touch. Remove from the oven and leave to rest for 10 minutes.

Meanwhile, make the watercress sauce. Melt the butter in a pan, stir in the flour and cook for 1-2 minutes. Remove from the heat and gradually stir in the fish fumet. Bring to a simmer, stirring, and cook, stirring, for 2-3 minutes until thickened and smooth. Set aside a few watercress sprigs for garnish; finely chop the rest and stir into the sauce; keep warm.

Remove the greaseproof paper from the moulds. Invert, one at a time, onto a plate, drain off any liquid, then invert onto a warmed serving plate. Soak up any remaining liquid with kitchen paper. Brush the turbans with melted butter and garnish with watercress. Serve with the watercress sauce and creamed potatoes.

CHOCOLATE GÂTEAU

6 eggs, size 3, separated
100 g (3½ oz) caster sugar
100 g (3½ oz) ground almonds
100 g (3½ oz) plain dark chocolate, grated

Topping:

100 g (3½ oz) plain dark chocolate, in pieces
300 ml (½ pint) whipping cream

Chocolate Caraque:

100 g (3½ oz) plain dark chocolate, in pieces

Grease a 20 cm (8 inch) loose-bottomed cake tin and line with greaseproof paper.

In a bowl, whisk the egg whites until they form firm peaks. Whisk in the sugar, 15 ml (1 tbsp) at a time. In another bowl, lightly beat the egg yolks, then gently fold into the whisked mixture. Add the ground almonds and grated chocolate and fold in lightly until evenly incorporated. Turn the mixture into the prepared cake tin and bake in a preheated oven at 170°C (325°F) mark 3 for 45 minutes. Allow to cool in the tin before turning out.

To make the chocolate caraque, melt the chocolate in a heatproof bowl over a pan of hot water, then spread in a thin layer on a marble slab or board. When the chocolate is just set, scrape off long curls by pushing a large knife across the surface of the chocolate.

To prepare the topping, melt the chocolate in a heatproof bowl over a pan of hot water. Remove the bowl from the heat and leave to cool slightly. In a bowl, whip the cream until it holds its shape, then fold in the cooled melted chocolate until evenly incorporated.

Spread the chocolate cream over the top and sides of the cake. Decorate with the chocolate caraque.

THE SECOND
SEMI-FINAL
ROSS BURDEN • TONY DAVIS • HELEN WELLER

HELLEN WELLER'S MENU

STARTER
Scallops with Lentil and Coriander Sauce
"CARDAMOM GOES WONDERFULLY WELL WITH FISH" JOSCELINE DIMBLEBY

MAIN COURSE
Hare in Green Pepper Sauce
Potatoes Olga
Braised Red Cabbage
Celeriac Purée

"THE HARE WAS DELICIOUS... ALMOST A GRAINY QUALITY AGAINST
THE TONGUE" STEPHEN FRY

DESSERT
Lemon and Ginger Hearts

"I ADORE SHARP LEMON PUDDINGS. THE CRISP BISCUIT BASE
WAS PERFECT" JOSCELINE DIMBLEBY

AND PUDDINGS SHOULD ALWAYS BE WHAT YOU WANT,
NOT WHAT YOU THINK YOU OUGHT TO LIKE" STEPHEN FRY

Brill en Papilotte with Fennel
ROSS BURDEN'S MAIN COURSE (FINAL)

Pan-fried Tenderloin of Tamworth Pork with a Prune and Armagnac Sauce
BRIAN TOMPKINS' MAIN COURSE (FINAL)

SCALLOPS WITH LENTIL AND CORIANDER SAUCE

12 large, very fresh scallops
15 ml (1 tbsp) sesame or groundnut oil
salt and freshly ground black pepper
15 ml (1 tbsp) lemon juice

Lentil and Coriander Sauce:
reserved scallop corals
300 ml (½ pint) chicken stock (approximately)
50 g (2 oz) puy lentils, soaked in cold water overnight and drained
15 ml (1 tbsp) sesame or groundnut oil
½ onion, sliced
1 large clove garlic, sliced
2.5 cm (1 inch) piece of fresh root ginger, chopped
5 ml (1 tsp) cardamom pods
2 large tomatoes, skinned, seeded and chopped, or 30 ml (2 tbsp) tomato passata
15 ml (1 tbsp) lemon juice
50 g (2 oz) unsalted butter, in pieces
15 ml (1 tbsp) crème fraîche, or soured cream
15 ml (1 tbsp) freshly chopped chives
15 ml (1 tbsp) chopped coriander

Clean the scallops, reserving the corals. Cut each scallop horizontally into 2 or 3 slices. Place in a bowl and add the sesame oil. Turn the scallop slices to coat in the oil. Season with salt and pepper; set aside.

To make the sauce, place the reserved scallop corals in a saucepan with 300 ml (½ pint) chicken stock and simmer for about 5 minutes. Strain the stock, discarding the corals.

Cook the lentils in boiling salted water until just tender, then drain.

Heat the sesame oil in a saucepan, add the onion, garlic and ginger and cook gently until golden. Meanwhile, remove and crush the seeds from the cardamom pods. Add these to the onion mixture off the heat and allow to cook in the residual heat for a few seconds. Add the tomatoes, two thirds of the cooked lentils and the strained stock. Season with salt and simmer for 10 minutes. Allow to cool slightly, then purée the mixture in a food processor or blender until smooth.

Return the lentil purée to the pan and reheat gently, adding a little extra stock as necessary to give a thick pouring consistency. Remove from the heat and gradually whisk in the lemon juice, butter, cream, chives and coriander. Stir in the remaining lentils; keep warm.

To cook the scallops; heat a dry frying pan until very hot, then add the scallops and fry quickly for about 30 seconds on each side. Drain on kitchen paper and sprinkle with lemon juice.

To serve, spoon a little of the lentil and coriander sauce on to each warmed serving plate and top with the scallops. Serve at once.

HARE IN GREEN PEPPER SAUCE

Prepare the stock for the sauce ahead, using the carcass from the hare.

15 g (½ oz) butter
1 saddle of hare, about 575 g (1¼ lb)
300 ml (½ pint) hare stock (see below)
30 ml (2 tbsp) whipping cream
5 ml (1 tsp) fresh green peppercorns
salt and freshly ground black pepper

Melt the butter in a frying pan, add the saddle of hare and seal briefly over a high heat, turning to brown on all sides. Transfer to a roasting tin and cook in a preheated oven at 200°C (400°F) mark 6 for 10-20 minutes, depending how rare you like it.

Meanwhile, put the hare stock in a saucepan and reduce by boiling vigorously until only about 60 ml (4 tbsp) remains.

Wrap the hare in foil and leave to rest for 5 minutes before carving into slices. Add the cream and peppercorns to the reduced stock. Check the seasoning and warm through; do not boil. Arrange the slices of hare on warmed serving plates and spoon over the sauce. Serve with the vegetable accompaniments.

Hare Stock: Break the hare carcass into pieces and place in a large saucepan with 1 onion, quartered; 1 carrot, quartered; 1 celery stick, roughly chopped; seasoning and a bouquet garni. Add sufficient water to cover. Bring slowly to the boil and simmer for 2-3 hours, skimming occasionally.

POTATOES OLGA

1 beef stock cube
16 new potatoes, scrubbed
15 ml (1 tbsp) olive oil

Dissolve the stock cube in 60 ml (2 fl oz) boiling water. Place the potatoes in a roasting tin. Pour in the stock and drizzle with the olive oil. Roast in a preheated oven at 200°C (400°F) mark 6 for 45 minutes or until tender, turning the potatoes and basting occasionally during cooking.

BRAISED RED CABBAGE

1 small red cabbage
2 onions, sliced
30 ml (2 tbsp) caster sugar
30 ml (2 tbsp) port
30 ml (2 tbsp) red wine vinegar
6 rashers streaky bacon, derinded and diced
1 bouquet garni
finely grated rind of 1 orange
salt and freshly ground black pepper

Quarter the cabbage, cut out the hard core, then shred finely. Place the cabbage in a flameproof casserole together with all the other ingredients and mix well. Bring to the boil, stirring. Cover tightly and cook in a preheated oven at 140°C (275°F) mark 1, for 2-3 hours until the cabbage is meltingly tender. Remove the bouquet garni and check the seasoning before serving.

CELERIAC PURÉE

450 g (1 lb) celeriac
125 g (4 oz) potato
salt and freshly ground black pepper
50 g (2 oz) butter, in pieces

Peel the celeriac and potato and cut into 2.5 cm (1 inch) cubes. Place in a saucepan and cover with cold salted water. Bring to the boil and simmer for about 15 minutes until tender. Drain well. Work to a purée using a food mill (moulé legumes) or potato masher. Beat in the butter and season with salt and pepper to taste. Serve immediately.

LEMON AND GINGER HEARTS

To make these, you will need 4 individual heart-shaped tins. These are available from kitchenware shops. Alternatively you could use heart-shaped biscuit cutters placed on a baking tray.

Bases:
150 g (5 oz) gingernut biscuits
65 g (2½ oz) butter, melted

Topping:
400 g (14 oz) can condensed milk
125 g (4 oz) packet full-fat soft cheese
* (eg Philadelphia)*
juice of 3 lemons
1 piece of preserved stem ginger in syrup

To make the bases, crush the ginger biscuits in a food processor, or between sheets of greaseproof paper with a rolling pin. Add to the melted butter and mix well. Divide the mixture evenly between the heart-shaped tins, pressing it on to the bases. Bake in a preheated oven at 180°C (350°F) mark 4 for 5 minutes. Allow to cool.

To make the topping, put the condensed milk, soft cheese and lemon juice in a bowl and whisk, using an electric beater, until the mixture thickens and is smooth. Finely chop the stem ginger and fold into the mixture.

Spread the lemon cheese mixture evenly over the biscuit bases and chill for 2-3 hours until firm. Carefully remove from the tins to serve.

THE THIRD
SEMI-FINAL
DEREK JOHNS • BETSY ANDERSON • KERRY CHURCH

WINNER

DEREK JOHNS' MENU

STARTER

Millefeuille of Salmon and Savoy Cabbage with a
Sabayon of Sherry

"IT LOOKED SIMPLE AND YET WHEN YOU CAME TO EAT IT THERE WERE
LOTS OF DIFFERENT THINGS GOING ON" VALENTINA HARRIS

MAIN COURSE

Stuffed Guinea Fowl Breast
Celeriac Rösti
Mangetouts
Carrots

DESSERT

Leche Frita

"THE DESSERT LOOKED LIKE A BEAUTIFUL PAINTING. IT WAS LIGHT
ON THE PALATE AND NOT SUPER SWEET" JAMES GALWAY

MILLEFEUILLES OF SALMON AND SAVOY CABBAGE WITH A SABAYON OF SHERRY

1 medium Savoy cabbage
salt and freshly ground black pepper
12 cm (5 inch) piece of salmon tail, about
  225 g (8 oz)
125 g (4 oz) butter, melted
250 ml (8 fl oz) dry white wine
lemon juice, to taste

Sabayon Sauce:
2 egg yolks
15 ml (1 tbsp) dry sherry

Remove the 4 outer leaves from the cabbage and discard. Carefully remove the next 16 leaves, cutting through the stalk of each leaf at the base and peeling off without tearing. Wash the leaves and pat dry with kitchen paper.

Using a 6 cm (2½ inch) pastry cutter, carefully cut out a round from each leaf. Reserve the rest of the cabbage. Add the cabbage rounds to a pan of boiling salted water and boil for 8 minutes. Drain and pat dry with kitchen paper. Put the leaves on a plate, cover and leave in the refrigerator for 10 minutes to firm up.

Meanwhile, prepare the salmon. Remove the skin and bones from the salmon tail, then slice the salmon flesh as thinly as possible.

Finely shred half of the remaining cabbage leaves, discarding the centre ribs. Put the shredded cabbage in a pan with 75 g (3 oz) of the melted butter and sweat for 2 minutes, stirring constantly. Add the white wine and cook gently for 10 minutes.

Remove from the heat and leave until cold, then press the mixture in a fine sieve over a bowl squeezing to extract the cabbage juices; reserve for the sauce. Keep the shredded cabbage for the millefeuilles filling.

To prepare the millefeuilles, set aside four dark green cabbage rounds for the top layer. To assemble each millefeuilles, brush a cabbage round with a little melted butter, cover with a fine layer of salmon, then add a squeeze of lemon juice and salt and pepper. Add a thin layer of cold shredded cabbage. Repeat these layers twice, then cover with a reserved dark green cabbage round, leaving the top cabbage round unbuttered. Assemble another 3 millefeuilles, in the same way.

To make the Sabayon sauce, put the egg yolks, sherry and 15 ml (1 tbsp) water in the top of a double boiler or in a heatproof bowl over a pan of hot water placed over a medium heat. Whisk constantly until the mixture thickens. Reheat the reserved cabbage juices and whisk into the sabayon, a little at a time. Season with salt and pepper to taste and keep warm.

Place the 4 millefeuilles in a steamer basket over a pan of boiling water and steam for 8 minutes. Carefully transfer to warmed serving plates and spoon on the sabayon sauce. Serve immediately.

STUFFED GUINEA FOWL BREAST

2 guinea fowl
2 carrots, finely chopped
4 shallots, finely chopped
2 garlic cloves, finely chopped
salt and freshly ground black pepper
120 ml (4 fl oz) Vin Santo (strong sweet
    Tuscan wine), or a sweet Sauternes wine
5-10 ml (1-2 tsp) chopped mixed herbs
    (thyme, rosemary and marjoram), to taste
pinch of dried oregano
1 egg

Garlic Butter:
25 g (1 oz) butter, melted
½ garlic clove, crushed

Beurre Rouge Sauce:
15 g (½ oz) butter
2 shallots, finely chopped
175 ml (6 fl oz) red wine
75-100 g (3-4 oz) butter, chilled and diced

Skin the guinea fowl, then carefully remove the breasts by slicing down each carcass from the breastbone; set aside. Strip the flesh from the wings, legs and carcasses, discarding any fatty tissue. Chop this meat for the stuffing.

To prepare the stuffing, sprinkle the chopped carrots, shallots and garlic over the base of a baking dish. Add the reserved chopped guinea fowl flesh. Season with salt and pepper and sprinkle with 60 ml (2 fl oz) of the wine. Cover and cook in a preheated oven at 180°C (350°F) mark 4 for 15 minutes.

Allow the mixture to cool slightly, then transfer to a food processor. Add the herbs and egg and work to a coarse cream.

To prepare each guinea fowl breast, hold down on the work surface with one hand and, using a sharp knife, slice into the breast horizontally to make a pocket, but do not cut right through. Open up

carefully, then place in a polythene bag or cover with a sheet of greaseproof paper. Beat with a meat mallet or rolling pin until it is almost 12 cm (5 inches) in diameter, without splitting in half.

Mound 2 tablespoonfuls of the stuffing into each pocket, then roll up and tie neatly with string; reserve the remaining stuffing. Put the guinea fowl breasts in the baking dish (used for the stuffing).

For the garlic butter, mix the melted butter with the garlic. Brush the guinea fowl breasts with garlic butter and season with salt and pepper. Sprinkle with the remaining wine. Cook in the oven at 180°C (350°F) mark 4 for 20 minutes.

To make the beurre rouge sauce, melt the butter in a pan, add the shallots and sauté gently for 2 minutes. Meanwhile press the reserved stuffing through a fine sieve to extract the juices. Add this liquid to the pan with the red wine and bring to the boil. Boil the sauce until it is well reduced and the shallots are just visible.

Remove the pan from the heat and whisk in the butter a piece at a time, making sure each piece is thoroughly incorporated before adding the next. Continue whisking until the sauce is the consistency of mayonnaise.

Remove the string from the guinea fowl breasts and replace with blanched chive strips. Place on warmed serving plates and spoon on the sauce. Serve immediately, with the celeriac rösti, mangetouts and carrots.

CELERIAC RÖSTI

1 celeriac
salt and freshly ground black pepper
25 g (1 oz) butter

Peel and quarter the celeriac, then grate coarsely into a bowl. Season with salt and pepper. Divide the mixture into 4 portions. Press each portion into a muffin ring or 7.5 cm (3 inch) plain metal cutter, resting on a fish slice or spatula.

Melt the butter in a frying pan and carefully slide the rings into the pan. Press the celeriac well down in the rings and fry for 3-4 minutes until crisp and golden brown underneath.

Turn the rösti, carefully remove the rings and cook the other side for 3-4 minutes until golden brown and cooked through. Drain on kitchen paper.

LECHE FRITA

525 ml (18 fl oz) milk
grated rind of ½ lemon
1 cinnamon stick
5 ml (1 tsp) vanilla essence
2 eggs, size 1
2 egg yolks, size 1
125 g (4 oz) granulated sugar
75 g (3 oz) plain flour
1 egg, beaten, for coating
50 g (2 oz) homemade dried breadcrumbs
  (see note)
corn oil, for shallow-frying
30 ml (2 tbsp) icing sugar (approximately)
2.5 ml (½ tsp) ground cinnamon

Fruit Coulis:
2 ripe mangoes
225 g (8 oz) raspberries

Put the milk in a saucepan with the lemon rind, cinnamon and vanilla. Bring slowly to the boil, remove from the heat and leave to infuse for 10 minutes.

Meanwhile in a bowl, whisk the eggs, egg yolks, sugar and flour together to a thick, smooth cream. Strain the milk through a fine sieve into the whisked egg mixture, stirring constantly. Return to the clean pan and bring to the boil, stirring constantly. Cook, stirring, for 3 minutes, until thickened and smooth.

Pour the custard into a well buttered square shallow dish of suitable dimensions to give a 2.5 cm (1 inch) depth of custard. Leave to cool for 1 hour, then refrigerate for at least 3 hours, until set firmly.

Meanwhile make the fruit coulis. Peel the mangoes and cut the flesh into chunks, discarding the stones. Put the mango flesh in a blender or food processor and work to a purée, then pass through a nylon sieve. Put the raspberries into the cleaned blender or food processor and work to a purée; sieve to remove the seeds.

Cut the firmly set custard into 5 cm (2 inch) squares. Dip each square into the beaten egg, then coat with the breadcrumbs, pressing them on firmly.

Heat a 2.5 cm (1 inch) depth of oil in a deep frying pan. Fry the coated squares in batches, turning, until browned on all sides, taking care to avoid breaking the crisp skin. Drain on kitchen paper.

Sift the icing sugar with the cinnamon then dip the *leche frita* in the cinnamon sugar to coat.

To serve, spoon the raspberry coulis onto one side of each serving plate and the mango coulis onto the other side. Using a chopstick, carefully feather the edges of the two sauces together. Place the *leche frita* in the middle and serve at once.

Note: To prepare your own dried breadcrumbs put dry bread in the oven on the lowest setting until crisp, golden and well dried. Crush with a rolling pin.

THE THIRD
SEMI-FINAL
DEREK JOHNS • BETSY ANDERSON • KERRY CHURCH

BETSY ANDERSON'S MENU

STARTER
Char-sui Pork with a Sweet Bean Sauce

MAIN COURSE
Monkfish in a White Wine Sauce
Glazed Sweet and Sour Carrots
Stir-fried Broccoli with Ginger

"WONDERFUL MONKFISH. ABSOLUTELY FABULOUS – AND THE CARROTS
WERE JUST AMAZING" VALENTINA HARRIS

DESSERT
Banana Dumplings with a Ginger Sauce

CHAR-SUI PORK WITH A SWEET BEAN SAUCE

For this dish you will need a small meat hook to suspend the pork in the oven. The meat needs to be cooked at a very high temperature – make sure your oven is hot enough before you put the meat in.

1 pork fillet (tenderloin), about 400 g (14 oz)
salt and freshly ground black pepper

Marinade:
15 ml (1 tbsp) tahini (sesame paste)
45 ml (3 tbsp) dark soy sauce
30 ml (2 tbsp) sweet chilli sauce
45 ml (3 tbsp) golden syrup
15 ml (1 tbsp) black peppercorns, coarsely crushed
15 ml (1 tbsp) star anise, broken into pieces
7.5 ml (1½ tsp) sesame oil
30 ml (2 tbsp) rice wine (sake) or dry sherry
1 spring onion, chopped
3 slices fresh root ginger
1.25 ml (¼ tsp) Thai spices

Sweet Bean Sauce:
15 ml (1 tbsp) corn oil
2 cloves garlic, crushed
2 x 5 cm (2 inch) pieces fresh root ginger, crushed or grated
15 ml (1 tbsp) yellow bean paste
15 ml (1 tbsp) light soy sauce
10 ml (2 tsp) sugar
30 ml (2 tbsp) chicken stock

To Garnish:
8 star anise
shredded spring onion

To make the marinade, heat the sesame paste with the soy sauce, chilli sauce and syrup in a small pan over a low heat for 1 minute until evenly blended. Tie the peppercorns and star anise in a piece of muslin and add to the mixture with the remaining marinade ingredients and 250 ml (8 fl oz) water. Pour into a deep dish and allow to cool.

Trim the pork if necessary and lightly score the surface, making 4 or 5 shallow cuts along each side of the meat. Sprinkle with salt and pepper and add the pork to the marinade. Cover and leave to marinate overnight in a cool place, turning once or twice.

Remove the pork from the marinade, scraping off any excess. Insert a meat hook through one end of the tenderloin.

Hang the tenderloin from the top shelf of the oven preheated to 240°C (475°F) mark 9. Place a roasting tin below to catch the drips. Roast for 35 minutes, then remove the hook, cover with foil and leave the meat to rest for 10 minutes.

Meanwhile make the sweet bean sauce. Heat the oil in a pan, add the remaining ingredients and cook, stirring, over a moderate heat for 5 minutes.

To serve, carve the char-sui pork into slices and arrange on warmed serving plates. Spoon over a little of the sauce and garnish with star anise and shredded spring onion.

MONKFISH IN A WHITE WINE SAUCE

450 g (1 lb) monkfish fillet
5 ml (1 tsp) salt
15 ml (1 tbsp) cornflour
2 egg whites
300 ml (½ pint) corn oil

White Wine Sauce:

2 slices of fresh root ginger, crushed,
    juice reserved
60 ml (4 tbsp) dry white wine
60 ml (4 tbsp) chicken stock
2 cloves garlic, crushed
5 ml (1 tsp) sugar
15 ml (1 tbsp) cornflour

To Garnish:

shredded spring onion

Cut the monkfish into small cubes. Sprinkle with the salt, then dust with the cornflour to coat lightly. Lightly beat the egg whites in a bowl with 7.5 ml (1½ tsp) of the oil.

Heat the rest of the oil in a wok or deep frying pan over a moderate heat. When it is hot, fry the fish in batches. Dip the cubes of fish in the egg white mixture, one at a time to avoid them sticking together, then fry in the oil for 2 minutes or until crisp and golden on the outside and cooked in the middle.

Drain the fish on kitchen paper and keep warm while cooking the remainder. Pour off the oil from the wok and wipe clean.

To make the sauce, combine the ginger juice, wine, stock, garlic and sugar in the wok. Blend the cornflour with 45 ml (3 tbsp) water, add to the wok and bring to the boil, stirring. Reduce the heat and cook, stirring, for 1½ minutes until thickened.

Add the fish to the wok and heat through for 45 seconds. Serve at once, garnished with spring onion.

GLAZED SWEET AND SOUR CARROTS

450 g (1 lb) carrots
15 g (½ oz) butter
15 ml (1 tbsp) lemon juice
15 ml (1 tbsp) brown sugar
15 ml (1 tbsp) soy sauce
pinch of crushed garlic
1 star anise

Cut the carrots into batons, about 5 cm (2 inches) in length. Put them into a small pan and add the remaining ingredients. Pour in just enough water to cover the carrots. Bring to the boil and fastboil the carrots, uncovered, for 15-20 minutes until all the water has evaporated and the carrots are coated in a thick glaze. Discard the star anise before serving the carrots.

STIR-FRIED BROCCOLI WITH GINGER

450 g (1 lb) broccoli
salt
30 ml (2 tbsp) corn oil
1 clove garlic, thinly sliced
2.5 cm (1 inch) piece fresh root ginger, finely
    shredded
2.5 ml (½ tsp) sesame oil

Separate the broccoli spears into florets and cut the base of the stems diagonally to give a neat appearance. Blanch in a saucepan of boiling salted water for 30 seconds. Drain and refresh in cold water; drain thoroughly.

Heat the oil in a wok or frying pan, add the garlic and ginger and stir-fry for 30 seconds. Add the broccoli and stir-fry for 2 minutes.

Sprinkle over the sesame oil and stir-fry for 30 seconds. Serve immediately.

BANANA DUMPLINGS WITH GINGER SAUCE

Banana Dumplings:
1 packet of filo pastry
2-3 bananas
20 ml (4 tbsp) light muscovado sugar
5 ml (1 tsp) ground cinnamon
melted butter, for brushing
25 g (1 oz) butter, in 4 pieces
30 ml (1 tbsp) chopped nuts (approximately)

Ginger Sauce:
30 ml (2 tbsp) sugar
large squeeze of lemon juice
2-3 pieces preserved stem ginger in syrup, sliced
30 ml (2 tbsp) ginger syrup (from the stem ginger jar)

To Finish:
icing sugar, for dusting

Cut twelve 12 cm (5 inch) squares from the filo pastry and keep covered with a damp tea-towel. Roughly chop the bananas and sprinkle with the sugar and cinnamon. Take 3 filo squares and brush with melted butter. Place them one one on top of the other, at an angle to each other and sprinkling chopped nuts between the layers.

Place a generous spoonful of the banana mixture in the middle of the top filo square and dot with a knob of butter. Gather the filo pastry up round the banana to enclose it and pinch together just below the corners to seal. Repeat to make 4 filo dumplings in total.

Place on a lightly greased baking sheet and brush with melted butter. Bake in a preheated oven at 180°C (350°F) mark 4 for 20-30 minutes until the pastry is crisp and golden.

Meanwhile make the ginger sauce, put the sugar in a pan with 60 ml (4 tbsp) water and heat gently until dissolved. Bring to the boil and boil until thickened and syrupy. Add the lemon juice, sliced ginger and ginger syrup to the pan and stir well.

Sprinkle the dumplings lightly with icing sugar and serve immediately, with the ginger sauce.

The Third
SEMI-FINAL
Derek Johns • Betsy Anderson • Kerry Church

Kerry Church's Menu

Starter

Terrine of Smoked Welsh Cheese with Walnuts

"THE CHEESE WAS DELICIOUS, REALLY WELL MADE, ESPECIALLY WITH THE WALNUTS" JAMES GALWAY

Main Course

Fillet of Sea Bass with Gooseberry and Nutmeg Sauce

Tagliatelle of Carrots

Broccoli Florets

New Potatoes

"THE SEA BASS WAS VERY SIMPLE AND WENT WELL WITH THE GOOSEBERRY SAUCE" JAMES GALWAY

Dessert

Cappuccino Ice Cream with Dark Chocolate Sauce

Langue de Chat Biscuits

"I VERY MUCH LIKED THE CAPPUCCINO ICE CREAM" LOYD

TERRINE OF SMOKED WELSH CHEESE WITH WALNUTS

If you are unable to obtain smoked Welsh goat's Cheddar, substitute a different smoked Cheddar cheese.

11 g (4 oz) powdered gelatine (1 sachet)
150 ml (¼ pint) apple juice
150 g (5 oz) smoked Welsh goat's
Cheddar cheese
25 g (1 oz) butter, softened
2-3 sage leaves, finely chopped
20 walnut halves, chopped

To Serve:
assorted salad leaves
wholemeal toast fingers

Sprinkle the powdered gelatine over the apple juice in a small heatproof bowl and leave to soak for 2-3 minutes. Stand the bowl over a pan of simmering water until the gelatine is dissolved. Remove from the heat and leave for about 5 minutes until cooled but not set.

Grate the cheese and place in a bowl with the softened butter and chopped sage. Mix thoroughly, using a fork.

Pour a thin layer of the apple juice mixture into a 300 ml (½ pint) terrine, to just cover the base. Place in the refrigerator until set.

Carefully spread half of the cheese mixture in the terrine, taking care to avoid damaging the jelly layer underneath. Sprinkle the chopped walnuts on top in an even layer, then pour on enough of the apple juice mixture to just cover them. Refrigerate until set.

Add the remaining cheese mixture and spread level, then top with the remaining apple juice mixture. Chill thoroughly for 2-3 hours if possible until set firmly.

To turn out, dip the base of the terrine into a bowl of hot water for a few seconds, then invert onto a plate. Cut into neat slices, using a knife dipped into hot water. Serve on individual plates, garnished with salad leaves and accompanied by wholemeal toast fingers.

FILLET OF SEA BASS WITH GOOSEBERRY AND NUTMEG SAUCE

Make sure that all scales have been removed from the sea bass fillets.

4 fillets of sea bass, each about 175 g (6 oz), with skin
melted butter, for brushing
salt and freshly ground black pepper

Sauce:
225 g (8 oz) fresh gooseberries, topped and tailed
150 ml (¼ pint) medium dry white wine
40 g (1½ oz) butter
2.5 ml (½ tsp) freshly grated nutmeg
soft brown sugar, to taste

First make the sauce. Put the gooseberries in a heavy-based pan with 45 ml (3 tbsp) water. Cover and cook gently over a low heat for 10-15 minutes until tender. Allow to cool slightly, then press through a nylon sieve to remove the skins and pips.

Return the gooseberry purée to the clean pan and add the wine, butter and half of the grated nutmeg. Bring to the boil, stirring occasionally, then add the remaining nutmeg and brown sugar, to taste; keep warm.

Place the sea bass fillets on a grill rack and brush with a little melted butter. Cook under a hot grill for about 8-10 minutes, depending on the thickness of the fillets, turning once during cooking. Season with salt and pepper to taste.

Arrange on warmed serving plates and spoon on the gooseberry sauce. Serve with the carrot tagliatelle, broccoli florets and new potatoes.

TAGLIATELLE OF CARROTS

225 g (8 oz) carrots
30 ml (2 tbsp) sunflower oil
25 g (1 oz) white mustard seeds
salt

Peel the carrots and, using a paring knife or potato peeler, pare the carrots into long thin ribbons to resemble tagliatelle.

Heat the oil in a small pan until hot, but not smoking. Add the mustard seeds and shake the pan for about 10 seconds only, until the seeds begin to pop. Immediately remove the pan from the heat, cover and wait until the seeds stop popping.

Add the "carrot tagliatelle" to the pan and mix well to coat in the oil. Cover and cook over a medium heat for 2-3 minutes; the carrots should retain some 'bite'. Check the seasoning, adding a little salt, if desired. Serve immediately.

CAPPUCCINO ICE CREAM, WITH DARK CHOCOLATE SAUCE

40 g (1½ oz) caster sugar
2 egg yolks
150 ml (¼ pint) cold strong black coffee
150 ml (¼ pint) double cream
150 ml (¼ pint) milk

Dark Chocolate Sauce:
50 g (2 oz) plain chocolate, in pieces
45 ml (3 tbsp) milk

Dissolve the sugar in 30 ml (2 tbsp) water in a pan over a low heat, then increase the heat and boil for 2-3 minutes. Allow the syrup to cool slightly. Whisk the egg yolks in a bowl until light in colour, then pour in the syrup in a steady stream, whisking continuously.

In a large bowl, whisk together the coffee, cream and milk until frothy. Gradually add this to the whisked egg mixture, whisking thoroughly.

Transfer the mixture to an ice-cream maker and churn for 15-20 minutes until thick and well chilled, but not frozen solid. Transfer to 4 chilled serving dishes and freeze until solid.

If you don't have an ice-cream maker, transfer the mixture to a shallow freezer-proof container and freeze for 2-3 hours until mushy. Turn into a bowl and whisk with a fork to break up the ice crystals. Refreeze until half-frozen, then whisk once more. Freeze in the serving dishes.

Meanwhile make the chocolate sauce. Melt the chocolate in a heatproof bowl over a pan of hot water or in the microwave on LOW. Whisk the milk into the melted chocolate until smooth. Leave to cool for about 15 minutes.

To serve, transfer the ice cream to the refrigerator about 15 minutes before serving to soften slightly. Pour on the chocolate sauce and serve with langue de chat biscuits.

LANGUE DE CHAT BISCUITS

Make your own vanilla sugar by storing a vanilla pod in a jar of caster sugar to impart flavour.

25 g (1 oz) butter
40 g (1½ oz) vanilla sugar
½ egg, size 3, beaten
25 g (1 oz) plain flour, sifted

Cream the butter and sugar together in a bowl until soft and light. Beat in the egg a little at a time, then fold in the flour.

Transfer the mixture to a piping bag fitted with a 1 cm (½ inch) plain nozzle. Pipe 7.5 cm (3 inch) lengths on a baking sheet lined with non-stick baking parchment, spacing them well apart.

Cook in a preheated oven at 220°C (425°F) mark 7 for 6-7 minutes until pale and golden. Leave on the baking sheet for 1 minute then, using a spatula, transfer the biscuits to a wire rack to cool completely.

Note: These biscuits can be made in advance and stored in an airtight tin, but they are at their best eaten within 24 hours of making.

THE
FINAL
DEREK JOHNS • ROSS BURDEN • BRIAN TOMPKINS

WINNER

DEREK JOHNS' FINAL MENU

STARTER

Pasta with Globe Artichoke and Wild Mushrooms

MAIN COURSE

Rosettes of Turbot with a Leek Sauce

"THIS DISH IS A LOT MORE COMPLEX THAN THE TITLE
SUGGESTS" SIR JOHN HARVEY-JONES

DESSERT

*Thin-crust Apple and Mango Tart with a Caramel and
Gingered Kiwi Sauce*

"THE DESSERT WAS A POEM" MICHEL ROUX

"REGARDLESS OF WHAT I PAID FOR THIS MEAL, I WOULD HAVE THOUGHT
I'D HAD REAL VALUE FOR MONEY" SIR JOHN HARVEY-JONES

TAGLIATELLE WITH GLOBE ARTICHOKE AND WILD MUSHROOMS

You will need a pasta machine to prepare the tagliatelle. If *pied de mouton* and *trompette de la mort* are unobtainable use other wild mushrooms, such as chanterelles, ceps or morels.

Pasta Dough:

100 g (3½ oz) strong plain flour
pinch of salt
1 egg, size 3

Sauce:

1 large globe artichoke
lemon juice, for brushing
25 g (1 oz) butter
60 ml (4 tbsp) extra-virgin olive oil
1 clove garlic, crushed
few drops of white truffle oil
salt and freshly ground black pepper
4 pied de mouton, cleaned
4 trompette de la mort, cleaned

To Serve:

freshly grated Parmesan cheese

To make the pasta, put the flour into a blender or food processor with the salt. Add the egg and process briefly until the dough holds together and forms a neat ball. Turn onto a lightly floured surface and knead until the dough is no longer sticky, about 8 minutes. Put the dough into a polythene bag and leave to rest in the refrigerator for 1 hour.

Divide the dough into 4 portions and flatten each one with your hand. Put it through the pasta machine, adjusted to the widest setting, dusting lightly with flour to prevent it sticking. Pass the dough repeatedly through the rollers, folding the sheet between each rolling and gradually narrowing the gap between the rollers so the dough is pressed firmly each time. When the rollers are set on the last but one notch on the handle, the dough should be silky smooth. Feed the pasta through the wider set of cutters to make tagliatelle.

Hang the tagliatelle up to dry for about 1 hour: either use a pasta dryer or hang the strips over a clean broom handle suspended between two chairs.

To prepare the artichoke, pull off the outside leaves and discard. Cut off the top 2.5 cm (1 inch), to remove the sharp tips. Slice the artichoke in half vertically and remove the choke. Rub the cut surfaces with lemon juice to prevent discolouration. Peel 2.5 cm (1 inch) of the stalk. Slice down through the artichoke very finely, so each slice includes parts of the stalk, heart and leaves.

To make the sauce, heat the butter and oil in a pan, add the artichoke slices and sweat gently over a low heat for a few minutes. Add the garlic and cook for a further 1-2 minutes. Add a few drops of truffle oil. Season with salt and pepper. Cut the wild mushrooms into long pieces, add to the pan and cook slowly for a further 1 minute.

To cook the pasta, have ready a large pan of boiling salted water. Add a few drops of oil, then add the tagliatelle and cook briefly for 1-2 minutes until *al dente* (tender but firm to the bite). Drain thoroughly.

Divide the tagliatelle between warmed serving plates and spoon over the artichoke and mushroom sauce. Serve immediately, with freshly grated Parmesan cheese.

ROSETTES OF TURBOT WITH A LEEK SAUCE

Ask your fishmonger to cut the piece of fish from the thickest part of the turbot, and skin and bone it for you. Reserve the bones for the stock; you will need to ask for more white fish bones to make up the quantity needed.

450 g (1 lb) turbot fillet, bones reserved
salt and freshly ground black pepper
juice of 1 lemon

Stock:
900 g (2 lb) fish bones
1 celery stick, chopped
2 shallots, finely chopped
1 leek (green leaves only), finely chopped
1 bay leaf
1 thyme sprig
salt
10 black peppercorns

Leek Sauce:
3 leeks (green leaves only)
2 large shallots, finely chopped
115 g (4½ oz) ice-cold butter, diced
120 ml (4 fl oz) Noilly Prat
120 ml (4 fl oz) dry white wine
15 ml (1 tbsp) double cream

Vegetable Garnish:
4 small courgettes
1 raw beetroot
½ cucumber

First make the fish stock. Put the fish bones into a large pan and add the remaining stock ingredients with 1.2 litres (2 pints) water. Bring to the boil and simmer for 30 minutes. Strain through a colander and return to the pan. Boil vigorously to reduce by half to 600 ml (1 pint). Strain the stock through a sieve lined with damp muslin into a bowl; set aside.

Using a very sharp knife, carve the fish at an angle into very thin slices. Season each slice and add a liberal squeeze of lemon juice to firm up the flesh.

Divide the turbot slices into 4 equal portions. Roll up the slices, overlapping each one to form a rosette. Secure each rosette with a cocktail stick and flay out the petals of the rosette to form a flower. Stand them in a steamer basket.

To make the sauce, finely chop the green parts of the leeks and blanch in boiling salted water for 3 minutes; drain. Melt 15 g (½ oz) of the butter in a pan and sweat the shallots gently for 2 minutes. Add the Noilly Prat, wine and reduced fish stock and boil to reduce by half.

Remove from the heat and whisk in the remaining butter, a piece at a time, making sure each piece is thoroughly incorporated before adding the next. When all the butter has been added, the sauce will be velvety smooth. Stir in the leeks and cream. Keep warm over a pan of hot water.

To prepare the vegetable garnish, cut the ends off the courgettes and cut the courgettes in half crossways, so that each piece is about 4 cm (1¼ inch) long. Stand upright and cut off four sides of the dark green skin, leaving a rectangle of flesh which you discard. Using a sharp paring knife, cut a fish shape out of each piece of skin (practice makes perfect).

Take the beetroot and cut four 5 mm (¼ inch) thick slices out of the widest part. Cut 8 small red fish shapes out of these.

Place the courgette and beetroot fishes in the steamer basket alongside the rosettes of fish.

Peel the skin off the half cucumber. Thinly slice the cucumber flesh lengthways into 5 mm (¼ inch) thick slices (avoiding the seeds and pulp). Cut these slices into strips, to form "cucumber spaghetti". Blanch in boiling salted water for 1 minute, then drain.

Place the steamer baskets of fish and vegetables over a pan of boiling water and steam for 2-3 minutes until the fish is white and firm.

To serve, carefully remove the cocktail sticks from the turbot rosettes. Place a rosette in the centre of each warmed serving plate. Pour around the leek sauce and garnish with the courgette 'fish', beetroot 'fish' and strips of cucumber spaghetti to resemble 'waves'. Serve immediately.

THIN-CRUST APPLE AND MANGO TART WITH A CARAMEL AND GINGERED KIWI SAUCE

4 firm Golden Delicious apples
lemon juice, for sprinkling
400 g (14 oz) packet puff pastry
2 fully ripened mangoes
50 g (2 oz) butter
350 g (12 oz) caster sugar
4 kiwi fruit
15 ml (1 tbsp) icing sugar
2 pieces preserved stem ginger in syrup, drained
250 ml (8 fl oz) double cream

Peel, quarter and core the apples. Using a swivel peeler, peel off thin strips of apple from each quarter – to give fine shavings. Sprinkle with lemon juice to prevent discolouration.

Roll out the pastry thinly on a lightly floured surface and cut out 4 rounds, 15 cm (6 inches) in diameter. Place the pastry rounds on a buttered baking sheet and prick all over with a fork.

Slice through each unpeeled mango on either side of the stone and cut the flesh into thin slices, then remove the skin from each slice. (Ripe mangoes are quite soft and the flesh cuts into thin slices more easily with the skin in place.)

Arrange alternate overlapping slices of apple and mango over the pastry rounds, starting at the edge and working towards the centre in a circular pattern. Dot the surface of each tart with butter and sprinkle with a little sugar. Bake in a preheated oven at 180°C (350°F) mark 4 for 12 minutes or until the pastry is cooked through. Remove from the oven and place under a preheated hot grill for 1 minute to caramelise the tops.

Meanwhile make a sugar syrup by dissolving 50 g (2 oz) caster sugar in 150 ml (¼ pint) water in a pan over a low heat. Bring to the boil and simmer for 4 minutes until thickened. Brush the surfaces of the warm tarts with the hot syrup.

To prepare the fruit sauce, peel the kiwi fruit and purée in a blender together with the icing sugar and stem ginger. Pass through a fine nylon sieve to remove the seeds.

Bring the cream to the boil in a saucepan. Meanwhile put the remaining sugar in a heavy-based pan with 15 ml (1 tbsp) water over a low heat until dissolved, then increase the heat and cook to a golden brown caramel. Very carefully add the caramel to the boiling cream (the mixture will splutter) and keep stirring over a low heat until the mixture is evenly combined.

To serve, place a tart in the centre of each serving plate. Pour the caramel cream sauce around one side of each tart and the gingered kiwi sauce around the other side. Serve warm.

THE
FINAL

DEREK JOHNS • ROSS BURDEN • BRIAN TOMPKINS

ROSS BURDEN'S MENU

STARTER

Stuffed Morels with Triangular Croûtes

"THE MORELS WERE BEAUTIFULLY TEXTURED, NOT CHEWY
OR CRUNCHY" LOYD

MAIN COURSE

Brill en Papilotte with Fennel and Truffle Oil
Parsnip Timbales with Asparagus and Broad Beans

DESSERT

Red and White Grapefruits with Candied Zests
"PERFECTION!" MICHEL ROUX

STUFFED MORELS WITH TRIANGULAR CROÛTES

24 fresh morels
squeeze of lemon juice
knob of butter

Stuffing and Sauce:
75 g (3 oz) butter
1 carrot, very finely chopped
1 celery stick, very finely chopped
4 shallots, very finely chopped
5 ml (1 tsp) very finely chopped thyme leaves
5 ml (1 tsp) very finely chopped parsley
170 ml (6 fl oz) port
120 ml (4 fl oz) double cream
15 ml (1 tbsp) fresh white breadcrumbs
1 egg yolk
salt and freshly ground black pepper

Croûtes:
2 large slices white bread
50 g (2 oz) butter
1 clove garlic, very finely chopped

To Garnish:
chopped parsley

Wash the morels very gently. Carefully cut off their stems and reserve, leaving the mushroom cavities intact. Put the mushrooms in a pan together with a squeeze of lemon juice, the butter and 600 ml (1 pint) water. Bring to a simmer and simmer very gently for 1 minute, then drain.

To make the stuffing, finely chop the reserved morel stems. Melt 25 g (1 oz) of the butter in a pan. Add the chopped morel stems, carrot, celery and half of the shallots, together with the chopped thyme and parsley and sauté for 2 minutes until softened.

Add half of the port and boil vigorously to reduce until only 15 ml (1 tbsp) of the liquid remains. Stir in 15 ml (1 tbsp) of the cream and all of the breadcrumbs. Remove from the heat and stir in the egg yolk. Season with salt and pepper to taste.

Transfer the stuffing mixture to a piping bag fitted with a small nozzle. Make a small slit in the side of each morel and carefully pipe the stuffing into each one until full.

To prepare the croûtes, remove the crusts from the bread, then cut each slice into 4 triangles. Heat the butter in a pan with the chopped garlic and fry the bread triangles on each side until golden brown. Drain on kitchen paper, then dip one corner of each croûte into chopped parsley, set aside.

Heat the remaining 50 g (2 oz) butter in a pan. Add the morels, together with the remaining shallots, cover and cook for 2 minutes. Add the rest of the cream and port. Continue to simmer, uncovered, for about 5 minutes, until the sauce has thickened enough to coat the morels.

Transfer the morels and sauce to warmed serving plates. Arrange 2 croûtes on each plate. Sprinkle with chopped parsley and serve immediately.

BRILL EN PAPILLOTE WITH FENNEL AND TRUFFLE OIL

Ask your fishmonger to skin and fillet the brill. For the papillotes you will need 4 large circles of baking parchment.

1 large brill, about 1.25 kg (2½ lb), skinned
  and filleted
2 small fennel bulbs
1 courgette
20 ml (4 tsp) olive oil
4 thyme sprigs
salt and freshly ground black pepper
40 g (1½ oz) butter
4 drops of truffle oil, or anchovy oil

Trim the 4 brill fillets as necessary and check that all bones have been removed.

Trim and slice the fennel and cut the courgette into julienne strips. Steam the vegetables for 5 minutes.

Heat the oil in a large pan and gently fry the brill fillets for about 1 minute on each side until browned but not cooked through.

To assemble the papillotes, cut 4 circles of baking parchment, each about 30 cm (12 inches) in diameter. Fold each circle in half, then open out flat. On one half of each circle form a base of fennel and courgette julienne. Lay a fillet of brill on top and add a sprig of thyme. Season with pepper and add a knob of butter and a drop of truffle oil.

Melt the remaining butter. Brush the other half of each circle with water to moisten. Brush the edges of the circles with melted butter to help them stick together. Fold the moistened half over the fish and fold the edges of the paper tightly to seal. Place on a baking sheet and bake in a preheated oven at 220°C (425°F) mark 7 for 7 minutes until the fish is cooked through.

Transfer the papillotes to warmed serving plates and serve at once.

PARSNIP TIMBALES WITH ASPARAGUS AND BROAD BEANS

900 g (2 lb) young parsnips
salt and freshly ground black pepper
1 clove garlic, finely chopped
5 ml (1 tsp) finely chopped thyme leaves
120 ml (4 fl oz) double cream
3 eggs, size 3, lightly beaten
1 red pepper
350 g (12 oz) shelled fresh or frozen broad
  beans
1 bunch of pencil-thin young asparagus
  spears
5 ml (1 tsp) butter
3 shallots, very finely chopped
250 ml (8 fl oz) crème fraîche

Butter 4 dariole moulds. Peel and quarter the parsnips, then remove the cores. Add to a pan of cold salted water and bring to the boil. Cook until tender, about 15 minutes; drain well.

Transfer the cooked parsnips to a food processor or blender and work to a purée. Add seasoning, garlic, thyme and the cream. Process briefly until evenly mixed. Transfer the mixture to a bowl and stir in the eggs.

Halve the pepper, discarding the core and seeds. Cook under a preheated hot grill until the skin is blackened. Place in a dish, cover tightly and leave until cool enough to handle, then peel away the skin. Cut one half into 8 strips, cut the other half into 16-20 small diamond-shaped pieces.

Place 2 red pepper strips on opposite sides of each dariole mould, then fill with the parsnip mixture. Cover each one with a circle of buttered greaseproof paper. Place the moulds in a roasting tin containing enough cold water to come halfway up the sides. Cook in a preheated oven at 220°C (425°F) mark 7 for 25 minutes until a skewer inserted into the centre comes out clean.

Meanwhile blanch the broad beans in boiling water for 3-4 minutes. Drain, refresh in cold water and drain again. Slip off the skins. Set aside about 24 broad beans for the garnish; keep warm. Steam the asparagus for about 8-10 minutes.

Meanwhile, to make the sauce, melt the butter in a pan and sauté the shallots until soft. Add the rest of the broad beans and sauté for 2 minutes. Stir in the crème fraîche and bring to the boil. Simmer for a few seconds. Pass through a fine sieve into a bowl; thin with a little water if necessary.

Unmould a parsnip timbale onto each warmed plate and arrange red pepper diamonds on the top. Surround with the sauce. Arrange the asparagus spears on the plates, interspersed with the reserved broad beans. Serve immediately, with the brill en papillote.

RED AND WHITE GRAPEFRUITS WITH CANDIED ZESTS

2 red or pink grapefruit
2 white grapefruit
450 g (1 lb) caster sugar
10 ml (2 tsp) clear honey

To Serve:
julienne strips of grapefruit rind

Using a sharp knife, peel and segment each grapefruit over a bowl to catch the juice, removing all white pith and pips. Add the grapefruit segments to the bowl of juice, then squeeze the membranes to extract all the remaining juice.

Using a sharp knife or swivel potato peeler, finely pare the zests from the grapefruit piths. Cut the zests into pieces, about 1 x 5 cm (½ x 2 inches). Put the grapefruit zest in a small pan, add cold water to cover and bring to the boil, then drain. Repeat this process twice more to remove the bitterness.

To make the sugar syrup, dissolve 350 g (12 oz) of the sugar in 120 ml (4 fl oz) water in a pan over a low heat, then bring to the boil. Add the zests, lower the heat and cook very gently in the syrup until they are translucent, about 20 minutes. Drain, discarding the syrup.

Dry the zests, then roll them in the remaining sugar to coat. Transfer to a wire rack and leave to dry for at least 30 minutes.

Drain the juice from the grapefruit segments and pour into a small pan. Add the honey and heat gently until dissolved. Allow to cool.

To serve, arrange alternate coloured grapefruit segments in a circle on each plate. Pour on enough of the sauce to cover the plate lightly. Decorate with the grapefruit zests.

THE
FINAL
DEREK JOHNS • ROSS BURDEN • BRIAN TOMPKINS

BRIAN TOMPKINS' MENU

STARTER
*Grilled Kiwi Mussels encased in a Sweet and
Sour Crunchy Topping*

MAIN COURSE
*Pan-fried Tenderloin of Tamworth Pork with a
Prune and Armagnac Sauce
Hasselback Potatoes
Parcels of Carrot and Celeriac wrapped in Savoy Cabbage*
"THE TAMWORTH PORK HAS GREAT DEPTH OF FLAVOUR" LOYD

DESSERT
*Upside-down Banana Pudding served with
Chocolate Custard*
"EXTREMELY GOOD!" LOYD

GRILLED KIWI MUSSELS ENCASED IN A SWEET AND SOUR CRUNCHY TOPPING

You can buy pre-cooked Kiwi or New Zealand greenlip mussels in their shells from fishmongers.

12 cooked Kiwi or New Zealand greenlip mussels in their half-shells

Topping:

15 ml (1 tbsp) sesame seeds
15 ml (1 tbsp) finely chopped bamboo shoots
15 ml (1 tbsp) finely chopped water chestnuts
7.5 ml (1½ tsp) finely chopped fresh root ginger
15 ml (1 tbsp) rice wine vinegar, or white wine vinegar
7.5 ml (1½ tsp) soy sauce
5 ml (1 tsp) oyster sauce
15 ml (1 tbsp) clear honey
finely grated rind and juice of 1 lemon
2.5 ml (½ tsp) five-spice powder
2.5 ml (½ tsp) paprika
salt and freshly ground black pepper

Mangetout Garnish:

12 mangetouts, topped and tailed
small knob of butter
pinch of five-spice powder

To Serve:

salad leaves
lemon wedges

To prepare the topping, toast the sesame seeds under a hot grill briefly until lightly golden. Set aside about a quarter. Put the remainder into a bowl and add the rest of the topping ingredients. Mix well and set aside to allow the flavours to mingle.

Meanwhile, loosen the mussels from the base of their half-shells with a sharp knife, but leave them in the shells. Put a teaspoon of the topping mixture on each mussel.

Place the mussels in a grill pan, and sprinkle with the reserved sesame seeds. Grill under a medium heat for about 4 minutes to ensure the mussels are heated through but stay moist.

Meanwhile, prepare the mangetout garnish. Cut the mangetouts into julienne strips. Heat the butter in a pan, add the mangetout strips and five-spice powder and stir-fry for 1 minute.

To serve, line individual plates with salad leaves. Arrange the hot mussels on the salad leaves. Garnish with the mangetout julienne strips and serve immediately, with lemon wedges.

PAN-FRIED TENDERLOIN OF TAMWORTH PORK WITH A PRUNE AND ARMAGNAC SAUCE

Tamworth is a particularly flavoursome breed of pig. If you are unable to obtain it, use any other well-flavoured pork.

2 pork tenderloins (preferably Tamworth),
about 350 g (12 oz)
salt and freshly ground black pepper
16 prunes (preferably Agen prunes)
600 ml (1 pint) good homemade chicken
stock
15 g (½ oz) clarified butter, for frying
120 ml (4 fl oz) Armagnac or brandy
150 ml (¼ pint) double cream

Season the pork tenderloins with salt and pepper. Put the prunes and stock in a pan and boil gently to reduce to just over 300 ml (½ pint). Remove the prunes with a slotted spoon and set aside half of them for the garnish. Remove the stones from the rest and pass through a sieve to form a purée, reserve the prune purée and stock.

Heat the clarified butter in a pan, add the pork tenderloins and sear over a high heat, turning to seal on all sides. Either transfer to a roasting tin and cook in a preheated oven at 225°C (425°F) mark 7 for about 10 minutes, depending on size, or continue to fry the pork in the pan, stirring frequently, until just cooked through but still moist.

Just before the tenderloins are fully cooked, pour on the Armagnac and set alight, shaking the pan to release the sediment on the base of the pan. When the flames die down, remove the pork from the pan, wrap in foil and leave to rest in a warm place for 5 minutes.

Add the reserved stock to the pan and boil vigorously until reduced to 150 ml (¼ pint). Stir in the prune purée to thicken the sauce and season with salt and pepper to taste.

Bring the cream to the boil in a separate pan and reduce by half. Add a tablespoonful of the purée sauce to impart colour. To serve, slice the pork and arrange on warmed serving plates on a pool of prune sauce. Pour on a little of the cream sauce and garnish with the reserved prunes. Serve immediately, with the vegetable accompaniments.

HASSELBACK POTATOES

8 medium Desirée potatoes
15 ml (1 tbsp) goose or duck fat
salt and freshly ground black pepper
1 bulb of smoked garlic, divided into cloves
1 bulb of fresh garlic, divided into cloves

Peel the potatoes and cut them in half crossways. Place flat-side down on a board and cut vertically into 5 mm (¼ inch) slices, but do not cut right through to the base. You should be able to flip the top like a deck of cards, while the bottom remains intact. Immerse the potatoes in a bowl of iced water and leave to soak for about 15 minutes. Drain and rinse under cold running water to remove as much of the starch as possible. Dry with kitchen paper.

Heat the fat in a roasting tin and add the potatoes, flat-sides down. Spoon the hot fat into the cuts, gently prising the slices apart. Season well with salt and pepper. Transfer to a preheated oven at 225°C (425°F) mark 7 and cook for 10 minutes. Add the garlic cloves and roast for a further 30 minutes, or until golden brown and tender, basting frequently.

PARCELS OF CARROT AND CELERIAC WRAPPED IN SAVOY CABBAGE

8 outer leaves of Savoy cabbage
6 large carrots
½ celeriac
25 g (1 oz) unsalted butter, melted
freshly grated nutmeg
salt and freshly ground black pepper

Blanch the cabbage leaves in a large pan of boiling water for 3 minutes, then drain and refresh in cold water; drain well. Cut each leaf in half through the centre, removing the tough stalk.

Peel the carrots and the celeriac and cut into matchstick strips. Blanch in boiling water for 3 minutes. Drain, refresh in cold water and drain again.

To assemble the parcels, brush the leaves with melted butter and season liberally with nutmeg, salt and pepper. Lay about 8 mixed vegetable matchsticks on one end of each leaf and roll up the leaf into a cigar shape, enclosing the vegetables.

Place in a shallow buttered ovenproof dish, seam-sides down. Brush with melted butter and season with salt and pepper. Heat through in a preheated oven at 225°C (425°F) mark 7 for 5 minutes.

To serve, cut each roll into 5 mm (¼ inch) slices and arrange cut-side down on the warmed serving plates.

UPSIDE-DOWN BANANA PUDDING

This pudding is best cooked in a frying pan which can be transferred to the oven. Alternatively, if you do not have an oven-proof frying pan, transfer the banana caramel to an ovenproof dish before adding the bananas and pudding mixture.

Pudding:
40 g (1½ oz) plain chocolate
25 g (1 oz) unsalted butter
30 ml (1 fl oz) double cream
3 egg whites
40 g (1½ oz) caster sugar
2 egg yolks, lightly beaten
25 g (1 oz) plain flour
15 g (½ oz) cocoa powder

Banana Caramel:
25 g (1 oz) unsalted butter
50 g (2 oz) caster sugar
60 ml (2 fl oz) crème de banane liqueur
2 ripe, firm bananas

Melt the chocolate in a heatproof bowl over a pan of hot water. Remove from the heat and add the butter and cream. Stir to mix, then set aside to cool.

Whisk the egg whites and sugar together in a bowl until firm peaks form. Using a large metal spoon, gently fold in the egg yolks. Sift the flour and cocoa powder together onto the mixture and lightly fold in, taking care to avoid losing all the air at this stage. Pour in the cooled melted chocolate and fold in gently. Set the pudding to one side while making the caramel.

To make the banana caramel, melt the butter and sugar together in a 20 cm (8 inch) ovenproof frying pan over a low heat, then increase the heat and allow to caramelise to a golden brown. Remove from heat and pour in the liqueur – take care as it will splutter. Stir well to mix. Cut the bananas into 5 mm (¼ inch) slices

and add to the caramel in a single layer.

Pour the pudding mixture over the banana caramel and cook in a preheated oven at 180°C (350°F) mark 4 for 15 minutes or until a skewer inserted into the centre of the pudding comes out clean. Leave the pudding to cool for 5 minutes, or longer if serving cold.

To turn out the pudding, loosen the edge from the pan by running a knife around, then invert a plate on top of the pan and turn over quickly. The pudding will turn out onto the plate with the caramelised bananas on top.

Serve hot or cold, with the chocolate custard.

CHOCOLATE CUSTARD

300 ml (½ pint) full-cream milk
1 vanilla pod
25 g (1 oz) plain dark chocolate, in small
  pieces
3 egg yolks
40 g (1½ oz) caster sugar

Pour the milk into a saucepan. Split the vanilla pod and scrape out the seeds. Add them to the pan together with the pod. Bring to a simmer and simmer gently for 3 minutes, then add the chocolate, remove from the heat and stir until melted.

Whisk the egg yolks and sugar together until the mixture is a pale straw colour. Pour on the hot milk mixture, whisking all the time, then return to the pan. Cook gently over a very low heat, stirring all the time until the custard thickens enough to coat the back of the spoon.

Pour the custard through a fine sieve and either return to the cleaned pan and keep warm over a very low heat until ready to serve, or set aside to cool if serving cold.

INDEX

OF RECIPE TITLES AND CONTESTANTS